THE OFFICE INBOX

JOKE BOOK

jokes for her

THE OFFICE INBOX

JOKEBOOK

jokes for her

First Edition

Edited by Jane Rooke

Printed in Sydney, Australia

Copyright © 2006

Drum Publishing

ISBN 1921263067

Published in Australia
by Drum Publishing
Erskineville, Sydney

www.drumpublishing.com.au

Text design and typesetting
by Louise Jackson-Moore

Cover image
by Louise Jackson-Moore

Layout & internal illustrations
Xou Pty Ltd
www.xou.com.au

Back cover pixel art from
www.istockphoto.com

Printed in Australia
by Ligare, Sydney

Contents

SUBJECT: AN AUSTRALIAN LOVE POEM

(Who said Australian men weren't romantic?)

Of course I love ya darling
You're a bloody top notch bird
And when I say you're gorgeous
I mean every single word
So ya bum is on the big side
I don't mind a bit of flab
It means that when I'm ready
There's somethin' there to grab
So your belly isn't flat no more
I tell ya, I don't care
So long as when I cuddle ya
I can get my arms round there
No sheila who is your age
Has nice round perky breasts
They just gave in to gravity
But I know ya did ya best
I'm tellin' ya the truth now
I never tell ya lies
I think its very sexy
That you've got dimples on ya thighs
I swear on me Nanna's grave now
The moment that we met
I thought u was as good as
I was ever gonna get
No matter wot u look like
I'll always love ya dear
Now shut up while the footy's on
And fetch another beer

SUBJECT: THE AMERICAN...

An American businessman was at a pier in a small coastal Mexican village when a small boat with just one fisherman docked.

Inside the small boat were several large yellow fin tuna. The American complemented the Mexican on the quality of his fish and asked how long it took to catch them. The Mexican replied, "Only a little while."

The American then asked why he didn't stay out longer and catch more fish?

The Mexican said he had enough to support his family's immediate needs. The American then asked the Mexican how he spent the rest of his time.

The Mexican fisherman said, "I sleep late, fish a little, play with my children, take siesta with my wife, Maria, stroll into the village each evening where I sip wine and play guitar with my amigos. I have a full and busy life, senor."

The American scoffed, "I am a Harvard MBA and could help you. You should spend more time fishing and, with the proceeds, buy a bigger boat.

"With the proceeds from the bigger boat, you could buy several boats, eventually you would have a fleet of fishing boats. Instead of selling your catch to a middleman you would sell directly to the processor, eventually opening your own cannery. You would control the product, processing and distribution.

"You would need to leave this small coastal fishing village and move to Mexico City, then LA and eventually NYC where you will run your expanding enterprise."

The Mexican fisherman asked, "But señor, how long will this all take?"

The American replied, "15 – 20 years."

"But what then señor?" asked the Mexican.

The American laughed, and said, "That's the best part! When the time is right, you would announce an IPO and sell your company stock to the public. You'll become very rich, you would make millions!"

"Millions, señor?" replied the Mexican. "Then what?"

The American said, "Then you would retire. Move to a small coastal fishing village where you would sleep late, fish a little, play with your kids, take siesta with your wife, stroll to the village in the evenings where you could sip wine and play your guitar with your amigos."

SUBJECT: AGEING

My body has become totally out of shape, so I got my doctor's permission to join a fitness club and start exercising. I decided to take an aerobics class for seniors. I bent, twisted, gyrated, jumped up and down, and perspired for an hour. But, by the time I got my leotards on, the class was over.

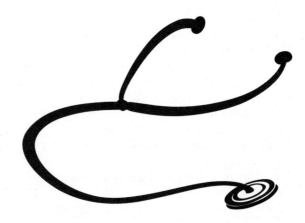

SUBJECT: ALZHEIMER'S TEST

Count the 'F's in the following text:

FINISHED FILES ARE THE RESULT OF YEARS OF
SCIENTIFIC STUDY COMBINED WITH THE EXPERIENCE OF
YEARS... (see below)

Managed it?
Scroll down only after you have counted them, okay?

How many did you get?

How many?

Three?

Wrong, there are six!! – No joke.

Read it again.

The reasoning is explained further down.

The brain cannot process 'OF'.

Incredible or what? Go back and look again!!

Anyone who counts all six 'F's on the first go is a genius.

Three is normal, four is quite rare.

SUBJECT: AIN'T THAT THE TRUTH

I was testing the children in my Sunday school class to see if they understood the concept of getting to heaven.

I asked them, "If I sold my house and my car, had a big garage sale and gave all my money to the church, Would that get me into Heaven?"

"NO!" the children answered.

"If I cleaned the church every day, mowed the yard, and kept everything neat and tidy, would that get me into Heaven?"

Again, the answer was, "NO!"

By now I was starting to smile.

Hey, this was fun!

"Well, then, if I was kind to animals and gave candy to all the children, and loved my husband, would that get me into Heaven?"

I asked them again.

Again, they all answered, "NO!"

I was just bursting with pride for them. "Well," I continued, "then how can I get into Heaven?"

A five-year-old boy shouted out, "YOU GOTTA BE DEAD."

SUBJECT: ANSWERING MACHINES

If you want to leave them wondering what the...

Messages for your answering machine.

1. A is for academics.
   B is for beer.
   One of the reasons is why we're not here. So, leave a message.

2. Please leave a message. However, you have the right to remain silent. Everything you say will recorded and will be used by us.

3. I'm probably home, I'm just avoiding someone I don't like. Leave me a message and if I don't call back, it's you.

4. Hello! If you leave a message, I'll call you back soon. If you leave a 'sexy' message. I'll call back sooner.

5. How dare you ring this number and expect someone to be here! We have places to go, people to see, and dinners to eat...

SUBJECT: BEST FRIENDS

After dinner and a movie, Carl drove his date to a quiet country road and made his move.

When Mary responded enthusiastically to his kissing, he tried sliding his hand up her blouse. Suddenly, she jerked away, got out of the car in a hurry, and ran home.

Later that night, she wrote in her diary, "A girls best friend are her own two legs."

On their next date, Carl returned to the country road. As they were kissing passionately, Carl slid his hand up Mary's skirt.

Once again, she pulled away, got out of the car and hurried home.

Later that night, she wrote in her diary, "I repeat, a girls best friend are her own two legs."

On the third date, the pair returned to the country road. This time, Mary didn't get home till very late.

That night, she wrote in her diary, "There comes a time when even the best of friends just part."

SUBJECT: THE BLONDE BIMBO

A ventriloquist is doing his act at the summer show and telling a few blonde jokes.

Suddenly, a blonde woman stands up at the back and shouts angrily, "You bastard, it's always the same, telling everyone that blondes are stupid. Well we're not."

"Look I'm sorry," says the ventriloquist, apologetically.

"It's just the act. I didn't mean to..."

"I'm not talking to you," interrupts the blonde heatedly, "it's that little bastard on your knee who's telling all the jokes."

SUBJECT: BUMPER STICKERS

Where there is a will... I want to be in it.

Friends help you move. Real friends help you move bodies.

As long as there are tests, there will be prayer in public schools.

"Women who seek to be equal to men lack ambition."

"Few women admit their age. Few men act it!"

Stop repeat offenders. Don't re-elect them.

A fool and his money are a girl's best friend.

Artificial intelligence usually beats stupidity.

My karma ran over your dogma.

What happens if you get scared half to death twice?

SUBJECT: LITTLE BOYS

A little boy got on the bus, sat next to a man reading a book, and noticed he had his collar on backwards. The little boy asked why he wore his collar that way.

The man, who was a priest, said, "I am a Father."

The little boy replied, "My Daddy doesn't wear his collar like that."

The priest looked up from his book and answered, "I am the Father of many."

The boy said, "My Dad has four boys, four girls and two grandchildren and he doesn't wear his collar that way."

The priest, getting impatient, said, "I am the Father of hundreds" and went back to reading his book.

The little boy sat quietly thinking for a while, then leaned over

And said, "Maybe you should wear your pants backwards instead of your collar."

SUBJECT: BECAUSE I AM MAN...

Because I'm a man, when I lock my keys in the car I will fiddle with a wire long after hypothermia has set in. The NRMA is not an option. I will win.

Because I'm a man, when the car isn't running very well, I will pop the hood and stare at the engine as if I know what I'm looking at. If another man shows up, one of us will say to the other, "I used to be able to fix these things, but now with all these computers and everything, I wouldn't, know where to start." We will then drink beer and break wind as a form of Holy Communion.

Because I'm a man, when I catch a cold, I need someone to bring me soup and take care of me while I lie in bed and moan. You're a woman. You never get as sick as I do, so for you this isn't a problem.

Because I'm a man, I can be relied upon to purchase basic groceries at the store, like milk or bread. I cannot be expected to find exotic items like 'cumin' or 'tofu'. For all I know, these are the same thing. And never, under any circumstances, expect me to pick up anything for which 'feminine hygiene product' is a euphemism.

Because I'm a man, when one of our appliances stops working, I will insist on taking it apart, despite evidence that this will just cost me twice as much, once the repair person gets here and has to put it back together.

Because I'm a man, I must hold the television remote control in my hand while I watch TV. If the thing has been misplaced, I may miss a whole show looking for it (though one time I was able to survive by holding a calculator)... applies to engineers mainly.

Because I'm a man, there is no need to ask me what I'm thinking about.

The answer is always either sex, cars, or football. I have to make up something else when you ask, so don't ask.

Because I'm a man, I do not want to visit your mother, or have your mother comes visit us, or talk to her when she calls, or think about her any more than I have to. Whatever you got her for Mother's Day is okay. I don't need to see it. And don't forget to pick up something for my mother, too.

Because I'm a man, you don't have to ask me if I liked the movie. Chances are, if you're crying at the end of it, I didn't... and if you are feeling amorous afterwards... then I will certainly remember the name and recommend it to others.

Because I'm a man, I think what you're wearing is fine. I thought what you were wearing five minutes ago was fine, too. Either pair of shoes is fine. With the belt or without it, looks fine. Your hair is fine. You look fine. Can we just go now?

Because I'm a man, and this is, after all, the year 2006, I will share equally in the housework. You just do the laundry, the cooking, the cleaning, the vacuuming, and the dishes, and I'll do the rest... like wandering around in the garden with a beer wondering what to do.

This has been a public service message for women to better understand the male.

SUBJECT: FINALLY, THERE ARE BLONDE MEN TOO

The Sheriff in a small town walks out in the street and sees a blonde cowboy coming down the walk with nothing on but his cowboy hat, gun and his boots, so he arrests him for indecent exposure.

As he is locking him up, he asks, "Why in the world are you dressed Like this?"

The Cowboy says, "Well it's like this Sheriff...

I was in the bar down the road and this pretty little red head asks me to go out to her motor-home with her... so I did.

We go inside and she pulls off her top and asks me to pull off my shirt... so I did.

Then she pulls off her skirt and asks me to pull off my pants... so I did.

Then she pulls off her panties and asks me to pull off my shorts... so I did.

Then she gets on the bed and looks at me kind of sexy and says, "Now go to town cowboy...
And here I am."

SUBJECT: BOOK REVIEW NEEDED?

PROBLEM:

Two books are for sale. Which to buy?
Titanic or *My Life* by Bill Clinton?

Titanic: $29.99
Clinton: $29.99

Titanic: Over three hours to read.
Clinton: Over three hours to read.

Titanic: The story of Jack and Rose, their forbidden love, and subsequent catastrophes.
Clinton: The story of Bill and Monica, their forbidden love, and subsequent catastrophes.

Titanic: Jack is a starving artist.
Clinton: Bill is a bullshit artist.

Titanic: In one scene, Jack enjoys a good cigar.
Clinton: Ditto for Bill.

Titanic: During ordeal, Rose's dress gets ruined.
Clinton: Ditto for Monica.

Titanic: Jack teaches Rose to spit.
Clinton: Let's not go there.

Titanic: Rose gets to keep her jewellery.
Clinton: Monica's forced to return her gifts.

Titanic: Rose remembers Jack for the rest of her life.
Clinton: Clinton doesn't remember Jack...

Titanic: Rose goes down on a vessel full of seamen.
Clinton: Monica... ooh, let's not go there, either.

Titanic: Jack surrenders to an icy death.
Clinton: Bill goes home to Hilary... basically the same thing.

SUBJECT: BBQ FUN

A woman was standing before the bedroom mirror, admiring herself in her expensive new outfit.

She posed this way and that before her husband, looking on with disinterest, remarked, "Your bum is the size of a three-burner barbecue!"

Later that evening, tucked up and cosy in bed, he lent over, tapped her on the shoulder, and asked hopefully, "How about it?"

She replied:
"It's hardly worth lighting the whole Barbecue for half a sausage."

SUBJECT: BRAIN CELLS...

Once upon a time there was a female brain cell which, by mistake, happened to end up in a man's head. She looked around nervously because it was all empty and quiet.

"Hello?" She cried, but no answer.

"Is there anyone here?" She cried a little louder, but still no answer.

Now the female brain cell started to feel alone and scared and yelled at the top of her voice, "HELLO, IS THERE ANYONE HERE?"

Then she heard a faint voice from far, far away...

"We're down here..."

SUBJECT: A BLONDE AND A LAWYER JOKE

A blonde and a lawyer are seated next to each other on a flight from Sydney to Melbourne. The lawyer asks if she would like to play a fun game. The blonde, tired, just wants to take a nap, politely declines and rolls over to the window to catch a few winks.

The lawyer persists and explains that the game is easy and a lot of fun. He explains, "I ask you a question, and if you don't know the answer, you pay me $5, and vice versa." Again, she declines and tries to get some sleep.

The lawyer, now agitated, says, "Okay, if you don't know the answer you pay me $5, and if I don't know the answer, I will pay you $500." This catches the blonde's attention and, figuring there will be no end to this torment unless she plays, agrees to the game.

The lawyer asks the first question. "What's the distance from the earth to the moon?"

The blonde doesn't say a word, reaches into her purse, pulls out a $5 bill and hands it to the lawyer.

"Okay" says the lawyer, "your turn."

She asks the lawyer, "What goes up a hill with three legs and comes down with four legs?"

The lawyer, puzzled, takes out his laptop computer and searches all his references, no answer. He taps into the air phone with his modem and searches the net and the library of congress, no answer.

Frustrated, he sends email to all his friends and co-workers, to no avail. After an hour, he wakes the blonde, and hands her $500.

The blonde says, "Thank you," and turns back to get some more sleep. The lawyer, who is more than a little miffed, wakes the blonde and asks, "Well, what's the answer?"

Without a word the blonde shrugs, reaches into her purse, hands the lawyer $5, and goes back to sleep.

SUBJECT: BILL AND HILLARY

Bill Clinton is getting $12 Million for his memoirs.

His wife Hillary, got $8 Million for hers.

That is $20 Million for memoirs from two people who for eight years repeatedly testified, under oath, that they couldn't remember anything.

SUBJECT: BOOM BOOM

A man and his wife were sitting in the living room and he said to her, "Just so you know, I never want to live in a vegetative state, dependent on some machine and fluids from a bottle. If that ever happens to me, just pull the plug."

His wife got up, unplugged the TV and threw out all of his beer.

SUBJECT: BLOKES AND WOMEN

Q: What is the difference between blokes and women.

A: A woman wants one bloke to satisfy her every need.
A bloke wants every woman to satisfy his one need.

SUBJECT: BLONDES

A blonde, down on her luck, decided to end it all one night by casting herself into the cold, dark waters of Fremantle Harbour.

As she stood on the edge of the dock, pondering her fate, a young sailor noticed her as he strolled by. "You're not thinking of jumping, are you?" he jokingly asked.

"Yes, yes I am" replied the blonde. Putting his arm around her, the kind sailor coaxed her back from the edge, "Look, nothing's worth that."

"I tell you what, I'm sailing off for Europe tomorrow. Why don't you stow away on board and start a new life over there. I'll set you up in one of the lifeboats on the deck, bring you food and water every night, and I'll look after you if you 'look after' me."

The blonde, having no better prospects agreed and the sailor snuck her on board that night. For the next three weeks the sailor would come to her lifeboat every night, bringing food and water and making love to her until dawn.

Then, during the fourth week, the captain was performing a routine inspection of the ship and its lifeboats. He peeled back the cover to find the startled young blonde and demanded an explanation.

The blonde came clean and shouted, "I've stowed away to get to Europe. One of the sailors is helping me out, he set me up in here and brings me food and water every night, and, and... he's screwing me."

The puzzled captain stared at her for a moment before a small grin cracked his face and he replied, "He sure is darlin', this is the Rottnest Ferry."

SUBJECT: COMPLETELY BANKERS

Shown below is an actual letter that was sent to a bank by a 96-year-old woman. The bank manager thought it amusing enough to have it published in the *New York Times*.

Dear Sir,
I am writing to thank you for bouncing my check with which I endeavoured to pay my plumber last month. By my calculations, three nanoseconds must have elapsed between his presenting the check and the arrival in my account of the funds needed to honour it. I refer, of course, to the automatic monthly deposit of my entire income, an arrangement which, I admit, has been in place for only eight years. You are to be commended for seizing that brief window of opportunity, and also for debiting my account $30 by way of penalty for the inconvenience caused to your bank.

My thankfulness springs from the manner in which this incident has caused me to rethink my errant financial ways. I noticed that whereas I personally attend to your telephone calls and letters, when I try to contact you, I am confronted by the impersonal, overcharging, pre-recorded, faceless entity which your bank has become.

From now on, I, like you, choose only to deal with a flesh and blood person. My mortgage and loan repayments will therefore and hereafter no longer be automatic, but will arrive at your bank, by check, addressed personally and confidentially to an employee at your bank whom you must nominate.

Be aware that it is an offence under the Postal Act for any other person to open such an envelope. Please find attached an Application Contact Status which I require your chosen employee to complete. I am sorry it runs to eight pages, but in order that I know as much about him or her as your bank knows about me, there is no alternative.

Please note that all copies of his or her medical history must be counter-signed by a Notary Public, and the mandatory details of his/her financial situation (income, debts, assets and liabilities) must be accompanied by documented proof. In due course, I will issue your employee with a PIN number which he/she must quote in dealings with me.

I regret that it cannot be shorter than 28 digits but, again, I have modelled it on the number of button presses required of me to access my account balance on your phone bank service.

As they say, imitation is the sincerest form of flattery. Let me level the playing field even further. When you call me, press the buttons as follows:

1. To make an appointment to see me.
2. To query a missing payment.
3. To transfer the call to my living room in case I am there.
4. To transfer the call to my bedroom in case I am sleeping.
5. To transfer the call to my toilet in case I am attending to nature.
6. To transfer the call to my mobile phone if I am not at home.
7. To leave a message on my computer, a password to access my computer is required. Password will be communicated to you at a later date to the Authorised Contact.
8. To return to the main menu and to listen to options one through seven.
9. To make a general complaint or inquiry. The contact will then be put on hold, pending the attention of my automated answering service.

While this may, on occasion, involve a lengthy wait, uplifting music will play for the duration of the call.

Regrettably, but again following your example, I must also levy an establishment fee to cover the setting up of this new arrangement.

May I wish you a happy, if ever so slightly less prosperous New Year.

SUBJECT: BEING A BEAR

If you're a bear, you get to hibernate. You do nothing but sleep for six months. I could deal with that.

Before you hibernate, you're supposed to eat yourself stupid. I could deal with that too.

If you're a bear, you birth your offspring (who are the size of walnuts) while your sleeping and wake to partially grown, cute cuddly cubs. I could definitely deal with that.

If you're a mama bear, everyone knows you mean business. You swat anyone who bothers you cubs. If your cubs get out of line, you swat them too. I could deal with that.

If you're a bear, your mate expects that you will have hairy legs and excess body fat.

Yep, I wanna be a bear.

SUBJECT: A SMART BLONDE

A blonde walks into a bank in London and asks to see the Manager. She says she's going to Hong Kong on business for two weeks and needs to borrow £5,000. The Manager says the bank will need some kind of security for the loan, so the blonde hands over the keys to a new Ferrari. The car is parked on the street in front of the bank, she has the title and everything checks out. The bank agrees to accept the car as collateral for the loan.

The Manager and the tellers all enjoy a good laugh at the blonde for using a £200,000 Ferrari as collateral against a £5,000 loan. An employee of the bank then proceeds to drive the Ferrari into the bank's underground garage and parks it there.

Two weeks later, the blonde returns, repays the £5,000 and interest which comes to £15.41. The Manager says, "Miss, we are very happy to have had your business, and this transaction has worked out very nicely, but we are a little puzzled. While you were away, we checked you out and found that you are a millionairess. What puzzles us is, why would you bother to borrow £5,000?"

The blonde replies...

"Where else in London can I park my car for two weeks for only £15.41 and expect it to be there when I return?"

A smart blonde joke at last!

SUBJECT: THE BLONDE

A popular blonde cheerleader bounced into the local card shop, looked around, then approached the clerk.

"Do you have any, like, real special birthday cards?" she asked.

"Yes, we do," he replied. "As a matter of fact, here's a new one. It's inscribed, 'To the Boy Who Got My Cherry'."

"Wow, neat!" she squealed. "I'll take the whole box."

SUBJECT: BIRTH CONTROL PILL

An elderly woman went to the doctor's office. When the doctor asked why she was there, she replied, "I'd like to have some birth control pills."

Taken aback, the doctor thought for a minute and then said, "Excuse me, but you're 75 years old. What possible use could you have for birth control pills?"

The woman responded, "They help me sleep better."

The doctor thought some more and continued, "How do birth control pills help you sleep better?"

The woman said," I put them in my granddaughter's orange juice, and I sleep better at night."

SUBJECT: BOOM BA BOOM!

Far away in the tropical waters of the Caribbean, two prawns were swimming around in the sea – one called Justin and the other called Christian.

The prawns were constantly being harassed and threatened by sharks that inhabited the area. Finally one day Justin said to Christian, "I'm fed up with being a prawn. I wish I was a shark, and then I wouldn't have any worries about being eaten." A large mysterious cod appeared and said, "Your wish is granted," and 'lo and behold, Justin turned into a shark.

Horrified, Christian immediately swam away, afraid of being eaten by his old mate. Time passed (as it invariably does) and Justin found life as a shark boring and lonely. All his old mates simply swam away whenever he came close to them. Justin didn't realise that his new menacing appearance was the cause of his sad plight. While swimming alone one day he saw the cod again and he thought that perhaps the fish could change him back into a prawn. He approached the cod and begged to be changed back, and, lo and behold, he found himself turned back into a prawn.

With tears of joy in his tiny little eyes Justin swam back to his friends and bought them all a cocktail. (The punch line does not involve a prawn cocktail – it's much worse).

Looking around the gathering at the reef he realised he couldn't see his old pal. "Where's Christian?" he asked. "He's at home, still distraught that his best friend changed sides to the enemy and became a shark," came the reply.

Eager to put things right again and end the mutual pain and torture, he set off to Christian's abode. As he opened the coral gate memories came flooding back. He banged on the door and shouted, "It's me, Justin, your old friend, come out and see me again." Christian replied, "No way man, you'll eat me. You're now a shark, the enemy and I'll not be tricked into being your dinner."

Justin cried back, "No, I'm not. That was the old me. I've changed..."

"I've found Cod. I'm a prawn again Christian."

SUBJECT: BALLS UP

A man decides to have a face lift for his birthday.

He spends $10,000. And, is really happy with the result.

On his way home he stops at the local newsstand and buys a paper. Before leaving, he says to the vendor, "I hope you don't mind me asking, but how old do you think I am?"
"About 35," was the reply
"I'm actually 47," leaving the vendor feeling very happy.

After that he goes to Mc Donalds for lunch and asks the young lady behind the counter, the same question. To which the reply is 29. "I'm actually 47." This makes him feel really good.

While standing at the Bus Stop asks a little old lady the same question. She replies, "I'm 85 and my eyesight is going. But when I was young we had a sure way of telling a mans age. If I put my hands down your pants and play with you balls for ten minutes, I will be able to tell your exact age."

As there was no one around, the man thought what the hell, let's give it a go.

Ten minutes later the little old lady says, "Okay, it's done. You are 47."

Stunned the man says, "That was brilliant! How did you do that?"

The little old lady replies, "I was behind you in Mc Donalds."

SUBJECT: GOOD CATHOLIC JOKE...

Two priests were determined to make this a real vacation by not wearing anything that would identify them as clergy.

As soon as the plane landed, they headed for a store and bought some really outrageous shorts, shirts, sandals, sun glasses, etc. The next morning, they went to the beach, dressed in their tourist garb.

They were sitting on beach chairs, enjoying a drink, the sunshine and the scenery when a drop dead gorgeous topless blonde in a thong bikini came walking straight towards them. They couldn't help but stare. As the blonde passed them, she smiled and said, "Good morning, Father, good morning, Father," nodding and addressing each of them.

They were both stunned. How in the world did she know they were priests?

So the next day, they went back to the store and bought even more outrageous outfits. These were so loud you could hear them before you even saw them. Once again the two priests settled on the beach, in their chairs, to enjoy the sunshine. After a while, the same gorgeous topless blonde, wearing a string, taking her sweet time, came walking toward them.

Again she nodded at each of them, said, "Good morning, Father," and started to walk away. One of the priests couldn't stand it any longer and said, "Just a minute young lady."

"Yes?" she replied.

"We are priests, and proud of it, but I have to know, how in the world did you know we are priests – dressed as we are?"

She replied, "Father, it's me... Sister Mary Frances."

SUBJECT: CHEWING GUM

An Australian man was having coffee and croissants with butter and jam in a cafe, when an American tourist, chewing gum, sat down next to him.

The Australian politely ignored the American, who, nevertheless started up a conversation. The American snapped his gum and said, "You Australian folk eat the whole bread?" The Australian frowned, annoyed with being bothered during his breakfast, and replied, "Of course."

The American blew a huge bubble. "We don't. In the States we only eat what's inside. The crusts we collect in a container, recycle them, transform them into croissants, and sell them to Australia."

The American had a smirk on his face. The Australian listened in silence. The American persisted. "D'ya eat jam with the bread?"

Sighing, the Australian replied, "Of course." Cracking his gum between his teeth, the American said, "We don't. In the States we eat fresh fruit for breakfast, then we put all the peels, seeds, and leftovers in containers, recycle them, transform them into jam and sell it to Australia."

The Australian then asked, "Do you have sex in the States?" The American smiled and said, "Why, of course we do." The Australian leaned closer to him and asked, "And what do you do with the condoms once you've used them?"

"We throw them away, of course"

Now it was the Australian's turn to smile. "We don't. In Australia, we put them in a container, recycle them, melt them down into chewing gum and sell them to the United States. Why do you think its called Wrigleys?"

SUBJECT: CONDOMS

A young man goes into the chemist shop to buy condoms.

The pharmacist says the condoms come in packs of three, nine, or 12 and asks which the young man wants.

"Well," he said, "I've been seeing this girl for a while and she's really hot. I want the condoms because I think tonight is *the* night. We're having dinner with her parents, and then we're going out. And I've a felling I'm gonna get lucky after that. Once she's had me, she'll want me all the time, so you'd better give me the 12 pack."

The young man makes his purchase and leaves.

Later that evening, he sits down to dinner with his girlfriend and her parents. He asks if he might give the blessing, and they agree. He begins the prayer, but continues praying for several minutes. The girl leans over and says, "You never told me that you were such a religious person."

He leans over to her and whispers, "You never told me that your father is a pharmacist."

SUBJECT: CORPORATE LESSONS. THESE ARE GOOD...

Corporate Lesson One:
A man is getting into the shower just as his wife is finishing up her shower, when the doorbell rings. The wife quickly wraps herself in a towel and runs downstairs. When she opens the door, there stands Bob, the next door neighbour. Before she says a word, Bob says, "I'll give you $800 to drop that towel." After thinking for a moment, the woman drops her towel and stands naked in front of Bob. After a few seconds, Bob hands her $800 dollars and leaves. The woman wraps back up in the towel and goes back upstairs. When she gets to the bathroom, her husband asks, "Who was that?" "It was Bob the next door neighbour," she replies. "Great!" the husband says, "did he say anything about the $800 he owes me?"

Moral of the story:
If you share critical information pertaining to credit and risk with your shareholders in time, you may be in a position to prevent avoidable exposure.

Corporate Lesson Two:
A priest offered a lift to a Nun. She got in and crossed her legs, forcing her gown to reveal a leg. The priest nearly had an accident. After controlling the car, he stealthily slid his hand up her leg. The nun said, "Father, remember Psalm 129?" The priest removed his hand. But, changing gears, he let his hand slide up her leg again. The nun once again said, "Father, remember Psalm 129?" The priest apologised, "Sorry sister but the flesh is weak." Arriving at the convent, the nun went on her way. On his arrival at the church, the priest rushed to look up Psalm 129. It said, "Go forth and seek, further up, you will find glory."

Moral of the story:
If you are not well informed in your job, you might miss a great opportunity.

Corporate Lesson Three:
A sales rep, an administration clerk, and the manager are walking to lunch when they find an antique oil lamp. They rub it and a Genie comes out. The Genie says, "I'll give each of you just one wish." "Me first! Me first!" says the administration. clerk. "I want to be in the Bahamas, driving a speedboat, without a care in the world." Poof!

She's gone. "Me next! Me next!" says the sales rep. "I want to be in Hawaii, relaxing on the beach with my personal masseuse, an endless supply of Pina Coladas and the love of my life." Poof! He's gone. "OK, you're up," the Genie says to the manager. The manager says, "I want those two back in the office after lunch."

Moral of the story: Always let your boss have the first say.

Corporate Lesson Four:
A crow was sitting on a tree, doing nothing all day. A rabbit asked him, "Can I also sit like you and do nothing all day long?" The crow answered, "Sure, why not."

So, the rabbit sat on the ground below the crow, and rested. A fox jumped on the rabbit and ate it.

Moral of the story:
To be sitting and doing nothing, you must be sitting very high up.

Corporate Lesson Five:
A turkey was chatting with a bull. "I would love to be able to Get to the top of that tree," sighed the turkey, but I haven't got the energy." "Well, why don't you nibble on my droppings?" replied the bull. "They're packed with nutrients." The turkey pecked at a lump of dung and found that it gave him enough strength to reach the lowest branch of the tree. The next day, after eating some more dung, he reached the second branch. Finally after a fourth night, there he was proudly perched at the top of the tree. Soon he was spotted by a farmer, who shot the turkey out of the tree.

Moral of the story:
Bullshit might get you to the top, but it won't keep you there.

SUBJECT: CRABBY WOMEN...
OF COURSE WE ARE

We started to 'bud' in our blouses at nine or ten years old only to find that anything that came in contact with those tender, blooming buds hurt so bad it brought us to tears. So came the ridiculously uncomfortable training bra contraption that the boys in school would snap until we had calluses on our backs.

Next, we get our periods in our early to mid-teens (or sooner). Along with those budding boobs, we bloated, we cramped, we got the hormone crankies, had to wear little mattresses between our legs or insert tubular, packed cotton rods in places we didn't even know we had.

Our next little rite of passage (premarital or not) was having sex for the first time which was about as much fun as having a ram rod push your uterus through your nostrils (IF he did it right and didn't end up with his little cart before his horse), leaving us to wonder what all the fuss was about.

Then it was off to Motherhood where we learned to live on dry biscuits and water for a few months so we didn't spend the entire day leaning over Brother John. Of course, amazing creatures that we are (and we are), we learned to live with the growing little angels inside us steadily kicking our innards night and day making us wonder if we were preparing to have Rosemary's Baby.

Our once flat bellies looked like we had swallowed a watermelon whole and we pee'd our pants every time we sneezed. When the big moment arrived, the dam in our blessed Nether Regions invariably burst right in the middle of the mall and we had to waddle, with our big cartoon feet, moaning in pain all the way to the ER.

Then it was huff and puff and beg to die while the OB says, "Please stop screaming, Mrs Hearmeroar. Calm down and push. Just one more good push (more like ten)," warranting a strong, well deserved impulse to punch the %*!* (and hubby) square in the nose for making us cram a wiggling, mushroom-headed ten pound bowling ball through a keyhole.

After that, it was time to raise those angels only to find that when all that 'cute' wears off, the beautiful little darlings morphed into walking, jabbering, wet, gooey, snot-blowing, life-sucking little poop machines.

Then come their 'Teen Years'. Need I say more?

When the kids are almost grown, we women hit our voracious sexual prime in our early 40s – while hubby had his somewhere around his 18th birthday.

So we progress into the grand finale, 'The Menopause', the Grandmother of all womanhood. It's either take HRT and chance cancer in those now seasoned, 'buds' or the aforementioned Nether Regions, or, sweat like a hog in July, wash your sheets and pillowcases daily and bite the head off anything that moves.

Now, you ask WHY women seem to be more spiteful than men, when men get off so easy, INCLUDING the icing on life's cake: Being able to pee in the bush without soaking their socks...

So, while I love being a woman, 'Womanhood' would make the Great Gandhi a tad crabby. Women are the 'weaker sex'? Yeah right. Bite me.

SUBJECT: CATS AND DOGS

This is why I have a dog, cats are too tricky.
Thought some of you pet lovers would get a smile from this

Excerpts from a Dog's Daily Diary:

7:00 a.m.	– OH BOY! DOG FOOD! BRILLIANT!!!
9:30 a.m.	– OH BOY! A CAR RIDE! BRILLIANT!!!
10:30 a.m.	– OH BOY! A WALK! BRILLIANT!!!
12:30 p.m.	– OH BOY! DOG FOOD! BRILLIANT!!!
1:00 p.m.	– OH BOY! THE YARD! BRILLIANT!!!
4:00 p.m.	– OH BOY! THE KIDS! BRILLIANT!!!
5:00 p.m.	– OH BOY! DOG FOOD! BRILLIANT!!!
7:00 p.m.	– OH BOY! PLAYING BALL! BRILLIANT!!!
9:30 p.m.	– OH BOY! SLEEPING ON MASTER'S BED! BRILLIANT!!!

Excerpts from a Cat's Daily Diary:

DAY 183 OF MY CAPTIVITY

My captors continue to taunt me with bizarre little dangling objects. They dine lavishly on fresh meat, while I am forced to eat dry cereal.

Pricks.

The only thing that keeps me going is the hope of escape and the mild satisfaction I get from ruining the occasional piece of furniture.

Tomorrow I may eat another houseplant.

Today my attempt to kill my captors, by weaving around their feet while they were walking, almost succeeded, must try this at the top of the stairs next time. In an attempt to disgust and repulse these vile bastards, I again induced myself to vomit on their favourite chair.

Note-to-self: I think I'll try crapping under their bed, too. Wonder how long it'll take them to find it?

Decapitated a mouse and brought them the headless body, to make them aware of what I am capable of, and to try to strike fear into their hearts. They only cooed and condescended about what a good little cat I was.

Damn! Not working according to plan.

There was some sort of gathering of their accomplices. I was placed in solitary throughout the event. However, I could hear the noise and smell the food. More importantly I overheard that my confinement was due to MY power of "ellergeez." Must learn what the bell this is and how to use it to my advantage. I am convinced the other captives are flunkies and maybe snitches.

The dog is routinely released and seems more than happy to return. He is obviously a bloody half–wit.

The bird, on the other hand, appears to have become an informant, and speaks with them regularly. I am certain he reports my every move. Due to his current placement in the metal room, his safety is preserved.

But I can wait, it's only a matter of time... little bastard

SUBJECT: IN THE CLASSIFIEDS

FREE YORKSHIRE TERRIER. EIGHT YEARS OLD.
HATEFUL LITTLE DOG. BITES.

FREE PUPPIES:
1/2 COCKER SPANIEL, 1/2 SNEAKY NEIGHBOUR'S DOG.

FREE PUPPIES...
PART GERMAN SHEPHERD, PART STUPID DOG.

GERMAN SHEPHERD 85 LBS. NEUTERED.
SPEAKS GERMAN. FREE.

FOUND: DIRTY WHITE DOG. LOOKS LIKE A RAT.
BEEN OUT AWHILE . BETTER BE A REWARD.

SNOW BLOWER FOR SALE... ONLY USED ON SNOWY DAYS.

COWS, CALVES NEVER BRED... ALSO ONE GAY BULL FOR
SALE.

NORDIC TRACK $300 HARDLY USED, CALL CHUBBY.

GEORGIA PEACHES, CALIFORNIA GROWN – 89 CENTS LB.

NICE PARACHUTE: NEVER OPENED – USED ONCE.

JOINING NUDIST COLONY!
MUST SELL WASHER AND DRYER $300.

OPEN HOUSE: BODY SHAPERS TONING SALON.
FREE COFFEE AND DOUGHNUTS.

FOR SALE: ONE MAN, SIX WOMAN HOT TUB

(AND THE BEST ONE) . . .

FOR SALE BY OWNER:
COMPLETE SET OF ENCYCLOPEDIA BRITANNICA NO
LONGER NEEDED. GOT MARRIED LAST MONTH.
WIFE KNOWS EVERYTHING

SUBJECT: GOTTA LUV THE SENIOR CITIZENS...

A tour bus driver is taking a group of seniors down a highway when he is tapped on the shoulder by a little old lady. She offers him a handful of peanuts, which he gratefully accepts.

After about 15 minutes she taps him on the shoulder again and she hands him another handful of peanuts.

She repeats this gesture about five times.

When she is about to hand him another batch, he asks the little old lady, "Why don't you eat the peanuts yourself?"

"We can't chew them because we've got no teeth" she replies.

The driver is puzzled and asks, "Why do you buy them then?"

"We just love the chocolate around them."

SUBJECT: CORONER'S REPORT

Three dead bodies turn up at the mortuary, all with very big smiles on their faces.

The coroner calls in the police to tell them what has happened.

First body, "Frenchman, 60, died of heart failure while making love to his mistress. Hence the enormous smile, Inspector," says the Coroner.

Second body, "Scotsman, 25, won a thousand pounds on the lottery, spent it all on whisky. Died of alcohol poisoning, hence the smile."

The Inspector asked, "What of the third body?"

"Ah," says the coroner, "This is the most unusual one: Big Seamus O'Quinn from Donegal, age 30, struck by lightning."

"Why is he smiling then?" inquires the Inspector.

"Thought he was having his photo taken !!"

SUBJECT: CHRISTIAN PUPPIES

A Baptist couple decide that they want to get a dog. As they are walking down the street in town, they notice that a sign in the pet shop is advertising 'Christian Puppies'. Their interest piqued, they go inside.

"How do you know they're Christian puppies?"

"Watch," says the owner, as he takes one of the dogs and says, "Fetch the Bible." The dog runs over to the desk, and grabs the Bible in its mouth and returns. Putting the Bible on the floor, the owner says, "Find Psalm 23." The dog flips pages with its paw until he reaches the right page, and then stops. Amazed and delighted, the couple purchase the dog and head home.

That evening, they invite some friends over and show them the dog, having him run through his Psalm 23 routine. Impressed, one of the visitors asks, "Does he also know 'regular' commands?"

"Gee, we don't know. We didn't ask," replies the husband.

Turning to the dog, he says, "Sit." The dog sits. He says, "Lie down." The dog lies down. He says, "Roll over." The dog rolls over.

He says, "Heel." The dog runs over to him, jumps up on the sofa, lays his paws for healing on the owner's forehead and bows his head.

"Oh look!" the wife exclaims. "He's Pentecostal!"

SUBJECT: CHILD SUPPORT AGENCY FORMS

The following are all replies that Dallas women have written on Child Support Agency forms in the section for listing fathers' name details.

1. Regarding the identity of the father of my twins, child A was fathered by Jim Munson. I am unsure as to the identity of the father of child B, but I believe that he was conceived on the same night.

2. I am unsure as to the identity of the father of my child as I was being sick out of a window when taken unexpectedly from behind. I can provide you with a list of names of men that I think were at the party if this helps.

3. I do not know the name of the father of my little girl. She was conceived at a party at 3600 Grand Avenue where I had unprotected sex with a man I met that night. I do remember that the sex was so good that I fainted. If you do manage to track down the father, can you send me his phone number? Thanks.

4. I don't know the identity of the father of my daughter. He drives a BMW that now has a hole made by my stiletto in one of the door panels. Perhaps you can contact BMW service stations in this area and see if he's had it replaced.

5. I have never had sex with a man. I am awaiting a letter from the Pope confirming that my son's conception was immaculate and that he is Christ risen again.

6. I cannot tell you the name of child A's father as he informs me that to do so would blow his cover and that would have cataclysmic implications for the economy. I am torn between doing right by you and right by the country. Please advise.

7. Peter Smith is the father of child A: If you do catch up with him, can you ask him what he did with my AC/DC CDs?

8. From the dates it seems that my daughter was conceived at Disney World, maybe it really is the Magic Kingdom.

9. So much about that night is a blur. The only thing that I remember for sure is Delia Smith did a program about eggs earlier in the evening. If I'd have stayed in and watched more TV rather than going to the party at 146 Miller drive, mine might have remained unfertilised.

10. I am unsure as to the identity of the father of my baby, after All when you eat a can of beans you can't be sure which one made you fart.

SUBJECT: COMPUTERS ARE DEFINITELY MALE...

Top eight reasons computers are male.

1. They have a lot of data, but are still clueless.

2. A better model is just around the corner.

3. They look nice and shiny, until you bring them home.

4. It's always necessary to have a backup.

5. They'll do whatever you say, so long as you push the right buttons.

6. The best part of having one is the games you can play.

7. Big power surges knock them out for the night.

8. Size does matter.

SUBJECT: BEST CHOCOLATE STORY EVER

It was a White Knight, and Mr. Cadbury and Ms. Rowntree were on a River Cruise. They met on the Top Deck. It was After Eight. She was from Quality Street, he was an Old Jamaican. They walked hand in hand down Milky Way and around the Family Block.

They stopped in at the Mars Bar, he had a Rum and Butter and she had a Wine Gum. She asked if he could pass her a Coaster, He said "Sure... take five." They Decided to leave as the music was too loud, and neither of them liked M and M.

On the way out he bought her some Roses. She said they were her Favourites. They walked down to his sports car, it was a Red Ferrero. He made some small talk, and tried to make out like he was a Smartie.

She spoke a little but didn't say much as she didn't want to Polly Waffle on. He suggested they should go somewhere quiet. She said if you play your cards right you might get lucky after tea. He replied, After Dinner?... Mint!"

At this point he knew she was Cherry Ripe! He asked her name. "Polo, I'm the one with the hole," she said. "And I'm the one with the Nuts" he thought. Then he touched her Milky Bars. They felt Smooth and Creamy. He thought to himself, They'll definitely melt in your mouth and not in your hand. He told her that he had a King Size Bar, but she thought he might just be telling Fantales.

They checked into a Motel and went straight to the bedroom. Mr. Cadbury turned out the light for a bit of Black Magic. It wasn't long before he slipped his hand down into her Snickers and felt her Kit Kat. She started to play with his Fruit and Nuts, but then she said, "Stop!" He thought she was a Malteaser, but he still wanted to Jaff-er. So he showed her his Curly Wurly.

Ms. Rowntree wasn't keen to have any more Jelly Babies, so she let him take a trip down Bourneville Boulevard. He thought this was Fantastic as he always fancied a bit of Fudge. It was a Magic moment as she let out scream of Turkish Delight. When he finished, his Fun Sized Mars Bar felt a bit Crunchie. She wanted Moro but he needed to take Time Out.

However he noticed her Pink Wafers looked very appetising... So he did a Twirl, had a Picnic in her Sherbet and gave her a Gob Stopper. He was exhausted, so he rolled over for a Flake.

Unfortunately Mr. Cadbury then had to go home to his wife, Caramel. Sadly, he was soon to discover he had caught V.D. It turns out Ms. Rowntree had been with All Sorts!!

SUBJECT: FOUR CATHOLIC LADIES

Four Catholic ladies are having coffee together, discussing how important their children are:

The first one tells her friends, "My son is a priest.
When he walks into a room, everyone calls him 'Father.'"

The second Catholic woman chirps, "Well, my son is a bishop.
Whenever he walks into a room, people say, 'Your Grace.'"

The third Catholic woman says smugly, "Well, not to put you down, but my son is a Cardinal. Whenever he walks into a room, people say, 'Your Eminence.'"

The fourth Catholic woman sips her coffee in silence.

The first three women give her this subtle, "Well...?"

She replies, "My son is a gorgeous, six foot two inches, hard bodied, well hung, male stripper.

Whenever he walks into a room women say, 'My God!'"

SUBJECT: OH NO... THE CHICKEN SURPRISE

A couple decide to go for a meal on their anniversary and after some deliberation decide on their local Chinese restaurant. They peruse the menu and finally agree to share the chef's special, 'Chicken Surprise'.

The waiter brings over the meal, served in a cast iron pot with a lid. Just as the wife is about to start in on the meal, the lid of the pot lifts slightly and she briefly sees two beady little eyes looking around before the lid slams back down.

"Good grief! Did you see that?" she asks her husband.

He hasn't so she asks him to look in the pot.

He reaches for it and again the lid lifts and he sees two beady little eyes looking around before it firmly slams back down.

Rather perturbed he calls the waiter over, explains what is happening and demands an explanation.

"Well sir", says the waiter. "What did you order?"

"We both chose the same", he replies. "The Chicken Surprise."

"Oh I do apologise, Sir, this is my fault..." says the waiter.

wait for it...

wait for it...

"I've brought you the Peking Duck"

SUBJECT: THE COMEBACK!!

If you ever testify in court, you might wish you could have been as sharp as this policeman.

He was being cross-examined by a defence attorney during a felony trial. The lawyer was trying to undermine the policeman's credibility...

Q: "Officer – did you see my client fleeing the scene?"
A: "No sir. But I subsequently observed a person matching the description of the offender, running several blocks away."

Q: "Officer – who provided this description?"
A: "The officer who responded to the scene."

Q: "A fellow officer provided the description of this so-called offender. Do you trust your fellow officers?"
A: "Yes, sir. With my life."

Q: "With your life? Let me ask you this then officer. Do you have a room where you change your clothes in preparation for your daily duties?"
A: "Yes sir, we do!"

Q: "And do you have a locker in the room?"
A: "Yes sir, I do."

Q: "And do you have a lock on your locker?"
A: "Yes sir."

Q: "Now why is it, officer, if you trust your fellow officers with your life, you find it necessary to lock your locker in a room you share with these same officers?"
A: "Well you see, sir – we share the building with the court complex, and sometimes lawyers have been known to walk through that room."

The courtroom erupted in laughter, and a prompt recess was called.

(The officer on the stand has been nominated for this year's 'Best Comeback Line' – and we think he'll win !!)

SUBJECT: CLUELESS HILLARY

Dear Abby,
My husband is a liar and a cheat. He has cheated on me from the beginning, and, when I confront him, he denies everything. What's worse, everyone knows that he cheats on me. It is so humiliating.

Also, since he lost his job six years ago, he hasn't even looked for a new one. All he does all day is smoke cigars, cruise around and bullshit with his buddies while I have to work to pay the bills.

Since our daughter went away to college he doesn't even pretend to like me and hints to people that I am a lesbian. What should I do?

Signed,
Clueless

Dear *Clueless*,
Grow up and dump him. Good grief, woman. You don't need him any more. After all you're a United States Senator from New York.

SUBJECT: CONFUCIUS SAYS...

"Virginity like bubble, one prick and all gone."

"Man who runs in front of car gets tyred."

"Man who runs behind car gets exhausted."

"Man who walk through airport turnstile sideways is going to Bangkok."

"Man who sleep in cat house by day, sleep in dog house at night."

"It takes many nails to build a crib, but only one screw to fill it."

"Man who farts in church, sits in own pew."

SUBJECT: CENTRELINK

A woman walks into the local Centrelink office, trailed by 15 kids...

"WOW," the social worker exclaims," are they ALL YOURS???"

"Yep they are all mine," the flustered Mother sighs, having heard that question a thousand times before. She says, "Sit down Leroy." All the children rush to find seats.

"Well," says the social worker, "then you must be here to sign up. I'll need all your children's names."

"This one's my oldest – he is Leroy." "OK, and who's next?" "Well, this one he is Leroy, also."

The social worker raises an eyebrow but continues.

One by one, through the oldest four, all boys, all named Leroy. Then she is introduced to the eldest girl, named Leroy.!

"All right," says the caseworker. "I'm seeing a pattern here. Are they ALL named Leroy?"

Their Mother replied, "Well, yes – it makes it easier. When it is time to get them out of bed and ready for school, I yell, 'Leroy!' An' when it's time for dinner, I just yell 'Leroy!' an' they all comes running." An' if I need to stop the kid who's running into the street, I just yell 'Leroy' and all of them stop. It's the smartest idea I ever had, namin' them all Leroy."

The social worker thinks this over for a bit, then wrinkles her forehead and says tentatively, "But what if you just want ONE kid to come, and not the whole bunch?"

"I call them by their last names."

SUBJECT: CIRCUMCISED – THIS IS PRICELESS!

A teacher noticed that a little boy at the back of the class was squirming around, scratching his crotch, and not paying attention. She went back to find out what was going on. He was quite embarrassed and whispered that he had just recently been circumcised and he was quite itchy. The teacher told him to go down to the principal's office.

He was to telephone his mother and ask her what he should do about it. He did it and returned to his class.

Suddenly, there was a commotion at the back of the room. She went back to investigate only to find him sitting at his desk with his penis hanging out.

"I thought I told you to call your Mum!" she said.

"I did," he said, "And she told me that if I could stick it out till noon, she'd come and pick me up from school."

KIDS, DON'T YOU JUST LOVE THEM???

SUBJECT: CHEESE SCONES

An elderly Irishman lay dying in his bed. While suffering the agonies of impending death, he suddenly smelled the aroma of his favourite cheese scones wafting up the stairs.

He gathered his remaining strength, and lifted himself from the bed. Leaning against the wall, he slowly made his way out of the bedroom, and with even greater effort, gripping the railing with both hands, he crawled downstairs.

With laboured breath, he leaned against the door frame, gazing into the kitchen. Were it not for death's agony, he would have thought himself already in heaven, for here, spread out upon waxed paper on the kitchen table were dozens of his favourite cheese scones.

Was it heaven? Or was it one final act of heroic love from his devoted Irish wife of sixty years, seeing to it that he left this world a happy man?

Mustering one great final effort, he threw himself towards the table, landing on his knees in a rumpled posture. His parched lips parted, he could almost taste the cheese scone before it was in his mouth, seemingly bringing him back to life.

The aged and withered hand trembled on its way to the nearest scone at the edge of the table, when his hand was suddenly smacked with a spatula by his wife, "Get lost!" she said, "They're for the funeral!"

SUBJECT: COFFEE IS BETTER THAN SEX BECAUSE...

- A long black is in fact long and black.

- A cappuccino is a guarantee of good head.

- You can always start the day with good coffee.

- Coffee keeps you up all night. Sex makes you sleep.

- Drinking coffee on your own doesn't make you feel like a sad loser (sex on your own does).

- You can make coffee last as long as you want.

- Coffee doesn't smell bad in the morning.

- You don't get into trouble for having coffee in front of your parents.

- Coffee doesn't care how many other cups you have had before.

- You can eat cakes and biscuits or other delightful treats while you have your coffee, but you can not do such luxuries while having sex.

SUBJECT: DAMN GOOD STORY...

Toward the end of the service, the Minister asked, "How many of you here forgiven your enemies?"

80 per cent of the congregation held up their hands.

The minister then repeated his question. All responded this time, except a small, elderly lady.

"Mrs. Jones? Are you not willing to forgive your enemies?"

"I don't have to," she replied. Smiling sweetly.

"Mrs. Jones, that is very unusual. How old are you?"

"98," she replied.

"Oh, Mrs. Jones, would you please come in front and tell us all how a person can live 98 years and not have an enemy in the world?"

Mrs. Jones, tottered down the aisle, faced the congregation and said:

"I outlived the bitches."

SUBJECT: DEAD PENIS

An old man, Mr. Smith, resided in the local nursing home.

One day he went to the nurse's office and informed Nurse Jones that his penis had died.

Nurse Jones, realising that Mr. Smith was old and forgetful decided to play along with him.

"It did? I'm sorry to hear that," she replied.

Two days later, Mr. Smith was walking down the halls of the nursing home, with his penis hanging out.

Nurse Jones saw him and said, "Mr. Smith! I thought you told me your penis died."

"It did" he replied, "Today is the viewing."

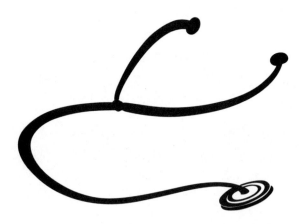

SUBJECT: DON'T FART IN BED

If this story doesn't make you cry from laughing so hard, let me know, and I will get someone to check your pulse.

This is a story about a couple who had been happily married for years. The only action in their marriage, was the husbands habit of farting in bed. Every morning the wife would plead with him to stop ripping them off, because it was making her sick. He told her, he couldn't stop it was perfectly natural. She told him to see a doctor as she was concerned that one day he would blow his guts out, because his habit of farting so loudly every morning when he woke. The noise would wake his wife, and the smell would make her eyes water, and gasp for air.

The years went by and he continued to rip them out! Then one Christmas morning as she was preparing the turkey for Christmas Lunch and he was upstairs sound asleep, she looked at the bowl where she had put the turkey innards, neck, gizzards, liver and all the other spare parts, a malicious thought came to her mind and a smile crept across her lips.

She took the bowl upstairs where the husband was sound asleep and gently pulling back the bed covers, she pulled back the elastic waistband of his boxers and carefully emptied the bowl of turkey guts into his boxers. Some time later she heard her husband waken with his usual trumpeting which was followed by a blood curdling scream and the sound of frantic footsteps as he ran to the bathroom. The wife could hardly control herself as she rolled around the floor laughing with tears running down her face, after years of torture she reckoned she had got him back pretty good.

About 20 minutes later her husband came downstairs in his blood stained boxers, he was pale with a look of horror on his face.
She bit her lip and asked, "What is the matter?"
He said, "Honey you were right all these years, you have been warning me, and I didn't listen."
"What do you mean?" asked the wife.
"Well you always told me that one day I would end up farting my guts out, and today it finally happened."
"But for the grace of god, some Vaseline and these two fingers, I think I got most of them back in."

SUBJECT: DIETING RULES...

1. If you eat something and no one else sees you eat it, it has no calories and therefore doesn't count.

2. When drinking a diet soda while eating a chocolate bar, the calories in the chocolate bar are automatically cancelled by the diet soda.

3. When you eat with someone else, calories don't count as long as you don't eat more than they do

4. Foods used for mechanical purposes never count. Example: hot chocolate, brandy, toast and cheesecake.

5. Any clear spirit, such as vodka or gin, is obviously the same as water and has no calories.

6. If you fatten everyone else around you, then you will look thinner.

7. If you are in the process of preparing something, any food licked off knives and spoons has no calories.

8. You can always move up a size and not tell anyone.

SUBJECT: DEFINITIONS FOR PARENTS

AMNESIA: Condition that enables a woman who has gone through labour to have sex again.

DUMBWAITER: One who asks if the kids would care to order dessert?

FAMILY PLANNING: The art of spacing your children the proper distance apart to keep you on the edge of financial disaster.

FULL NAME: What you call you child when you're mad at him.

GRANDPARENTS: The people who think your children are wonderful even though they're sure you're not raising them right.

HEARSAY: What toddlers do when anyone mutters a dirty word.

IMPREGNABLE: A woman whose memory of labour is still vivid.

INDEPENDENT: How we want our children to be as long as they do everything we say.

OW: The first word spoken by children with older siblings.

PRENATAL: When your life was still somewhat your own.

PUDDLE: A small body of water that draws other small bodies wearing dry shoes into it.

SHOW OFF: A child who is more talented than yours.

STERILIZE: What you do to your first baby's pacifier by boiling it and to your last baby's pacifier by blowing on it.

TOP BUNK: Where you should never put a child wearing Superman pjamas

TWO MINUTE WARNING: When the baby's face turns red and she begins to make those familiar grunting noises.

WHODUNIT: None of the kids that live in your house.

SUBJECT: DON'T

Don't ever leave the one you love for the one you like, because the one you like will leave you for the one they love.

SUBJECT: THINGS THAT ARE DIFFICULT TO SAY WHEN YOU'RE DRUNK...

Things that are difficult to say when you're drunk...
     a) Innovative
     b) Preliminary
     c) Proliferation
     d) Cinnamon

Things that are VERY difficult to say when you're drunk...
     a) Specificity
     b) British Constitution
     c) Passive-aggressive disorder
     d) Transubstantiate

Things that are ABSOLUTELY IMPOSSIBLE to say when you're drunk...
     a) Thanks, but I don't want to sleep with you.
     b) Nope, no more booze for me.
     c) Sorry, but you're not really my type.
     d) No kebab for me, thank you.
     e) Good evening officer, isn't it lovely out tonight?
     f) I'm not interested in fighting you.
     g) Oh, I just couldn't – no one wants to hear me sing.
     h) Thank you, but I won't make any attempt to dance, I have no co-ordination. I'd hate to look like a fool.
     i) Where is the nearest toilet? I refuse to vomit in the street.
     j) I must be going home now as I have work in the morning.

SUBJECT: OH DEAR...

Coming into the bar and ordering a double, the man leaned over and confided to the bartender, "I'm so pissed off!"

"Oh yeah? What happened?" asked the bartender politely.

"See, I met this beautiful woman who invited me back to her home. We stripped off our clothes and jumped into bed and we were just about to make love when her damned husband came in the front door. So I had to jump out of the bedroom window and hang from the ledge by my fingernails!"

"Gee, that's tough," commiserated the bartender.

"Right, but that's not what really got me," the customer went on, "When her husband came into the room he said 'Hey great! You're naked already! Let me just take a leak.' And damned if the lazy son of a bitch didn't piss out the window right onto my head?"

"Yeech!" the bartender shook his head. "No wonder you're in a lousy mood."

"Yeah, but I haven't told you what really, really got to me. Next, I had to listen to them grunting and groaning and when they finished, the husband tossed his condom out of the window. And where does it land? My damned forehead!"

"Damn, that's awful!" says the bartender.

"Oh, I'm not finished. See what really pissed me off was when the husband had to take a dump. It turns out that their toilet is broken, so he stuck his ass out of the window and let loose right on my head!"

The bartender paled. "That would sure mess up my day."

"Yeah, yeah, yeah," the fellow rattled on, "But do you know what REALLY, REALLY, REALLY pissed me off? When I looked down and saw that my feet were only SIX inches off the ground."

SUBJECT: ** WHAT IS THE DEFINITION OF **

Amnesia? What did you just ask me?

Apathy? I don't care.

Bigotry? I'm not going to tell someone like you.

Egotistical? I'm the best person to answer that question.

Evasive? Go do your homework.

Flatulent? That question really stinks!

Ignorance? I don't know.

Indifference? It doesn't matter.

Influenza? You've got to be sick to ask me that question.

Insomnia? I stayed awake all last night thinking of the answer.

Irreverent? I swear to God, you ask too many questions!

Narcissism? Before I answer, tell me, don't I look great?

Over Protective? I don't know if you're ready for the answer.

Paranoid? You probably think I don't know the answer, do you?

Procrastination? I'll tell you tomorrow.

Repetitive? I already told you the answer once before.

Self Centred? Well, I know the answer, that's all that matters.

Suspicious? Why are you asking me all these questions?

SUBJECT: DICTIONARY...
FOR ALL YOU MUM'S OUT THERE

AEROPLANE: What Mum impersonates to get a one-year-old to eat strained beets.

ALIEN: What Mum would suspect had invaded her house if she spotted a child-sized creature cleaning up after itself.

APPLE: Nutritious lunchtime dessert which children will trade for cupcakes.

BABY:
1. Dad, when he gets a cold.
2. Mum's youngest child, even if he's 42.

BATHROOM: A room used by the entire family, believed by all, except Mum, to be self-cleaning.

BECAUSE: Mum's reason for having kids do things which can't be explained logically.

BED AND BREAKFAST: Two things the kids will never make for themselves.

CHINA: Legendary nation reportedly populated by children who love leftover vegetables.

COOK:
1. Act of preparing food for consumption.
2. Mum's other name.

COUCH POTATO: What Mum finds on the sofa during football games.

DATE: Infrequent outings with Dad where Mum can enjoy worrying about the kids in a different setting.

DRINKING GLASS: Any carton or bottle left open in the fridge.

DUST: Insidious interloping particles of evil that turn a home into a battle zone.

continued...

ENERGY:	Element of vitality kids always have an oversupply of until asked to do something.
FABLE:	A story told by a teenager arriving home after curfew.
FOOD:	The response Mum usually gives in answer to the question, "What's for dinner tonight?"
GARBAGE:	Refuse items, the taking out of which Mum assigns to a different family member each week, then winds up doing herself.
GENIUSES:	Amazingly, all of Mum's kids.
GUM:	Adhesive for the hair.
HANDI-WIPES:	Pants, shirt–sleeves, drapes, etc.
INSIDE:	The place that will suddenly look attractive to kids once Mum has spent at least 30 minutes getting them ready to go outside.
"I SAID SO":	Reason enough, according to Mum.
KISS:	Mum's Medicine
LAKE:	Large body of water into which a kid will jump should his friends do so.
MAYBE:	No.
MILK:	A healthy beverage which kids will gladly drink once it's turned into junk food by the addition of sugar and cocoa.
OCEAN:	What the bathroom floor looks like after bath night for kids, assorted pets, two or three full-sized towels and several dozen toy boats, cars and animals.
OPEN:	The position of children's mouths when they eat in front of company.

SUBJECT: DOCTORS OFFICE

This is so true! They always ask at the doctor's office why you are there and you say in front of others what's wrong and sometimes it's embarrassing.

There's nothing worse than a doctor's receptionist who insists you tell her what is wrong with you in a room full of other patients. I know most of us have experienced this, and I love the way this old guy handled it.

An 86-year-old man walked into a crowded doctor's waiting room. As he approached the desk, the receptionist said, "Yes sir, what are you seeing the doctor for today?"

"There's something wrong with my dick," he replied. The receptionist became irritated and said, "You shouldn't come into a crowded doctor's room and say things like that."

"Why not? You asked me what was wrong and I told you," he said. The receptionist replied, "You've obviously caused some embarrassment in this room full of people. You should have said there is something wrong with your ear or something and then discussed the problem further with the doctor in private."

The man replied, "You shouldn't ask people things in a room full of others, if the answer could embarrass anyone."

The man walked out, waited several minutes and then re-entered.

The receptionist smiled smugly and asked, "Yes?"

"There's something wrong with my ear," he stated. The receptionist nodded approvingly and smiled, knowing he had taken her advice.

"And what is wrong with your ear, Sir?" The waiting room erupted in laughter.

"I can't piss out of it," the man replied.

SUBJECT: DUUUHHHHHHHHHHHHHH...

Pun Intended...

- I wondered why the baseball was getting bigger. Then it hit me.

- He drove his expensive car into a tree and found out how the Mercedes bends.

- Those who jump off a Paris bridge are in Seine.

- A cardboard belt would be a waist of paper.

- He wears glasses during maths because it improves division.

- Two peanuts were walking in a tough neighbourhood and one of them was a-salted.

- Did you hear about the guy whose whole left side was cut off? He's all right now.

- When the smog lifts in Los Angeles, U C L A.

- It was an emotional wedding. Even the cake was in tiers.

- Those who throw dirt are sure to lose ground.

- When the waiter spilled a drink on his shirt, he said, "This one is on me."

SUBJECT: POLISH DIVORCE

A Polish man moved to the USA and married an American girl.

Although his English was far from perfect, they got along very well until one day he rushed into a lawyer's office and asked him if he could arrange a divorce for him 'very quick'.

The lawyer said that the speed for getting a divorce would depend on the circumstances, and asked him the following questions:

LAWYER:	"Have you any grounds?"
POLE:	"JA, JA, acre and half and nice little home."
LAWYER:	"No, I mean what is the foundation of this case?"
	"Does either of you have a real grudge?"
POLE:	"No, we have carport, and not need one."
LAWYER:	"I mean, What are your relations like?"
POLE:	"All my relations still in Poland."
LAWYER:	"Is there any infidelity in your marriage?"
POLE:	"Ja, we have hi-fidelity stereo set and good DVD player."
LAWYER:	Does your wife beat you up?"
POLE:	"No, I always up before her."
LAWYER:	"WHY do you want this divorce?"
POLE:	"She going to kill me."
LAWYER:	"What makes you think that?"
POLE:	"I got proof."
LAWYER:	"What kind of proof?"
POLE:	"She going to poison me. She buy a bottle at drug store and put on shelf in bathroom. I can read, and it say, 'Polish Remover'."

SUBJECT: DECEASED

Two women were taking tea at the Ritz and catching up on family news.

"I'm sorry to hear your Stanley had died," remarked the first woman. "I hope you've been able to carry on life without him."

"Yes thank you," came the reply. "He was such a kind and thoughtful man. Do you know hours before he died he gave me three envelopes which he told me would ease the burden once he had gone."

"How thoughtful!" remarked the first woman. "What was in them?"

"Well the first had $2,000 in it to buy a coffin.

"The second had $3,000 in it and a note saying, 'This is to give me a good send off.' And let me tell you. They'll be talking about his funeral for years to come!"

"And what about the third envelope?"

"Oh, that said 'Use this cheque for $5,000 to buy a nice stone'."
"So I did," she said, holding out her finger to show a diamond ring, "what do you think of it?"

SUBJECT: THE PERFECT DRESS

Jennifer's wedding day was fast approaching. Nothing could dampen her excitement – not even her parents' nasty divorce. Her mother had found the PERFECT dress to wear and would be the best dressed Mother of the Bride ever!

A week later, Jennifer was horrified to learn that her father's new young wife had bought the exact same dress! Jennifer asked her to exchange it, but she refused. "Absolutely not, I look like a million bucks in this dress, and I'm wearing it," she replied. Jennifer told her mother who graciously said, "Never mind, sweetheart. I'll get another dress. After all, it's your special day."

A few days later, they went shopping and did find another gorgeous dress. When they stopped for lunch, Jennifer asked her mother, "Aren't you going to return the other dress? You really don't have another occasion where you could wear it." Her mother just smiled and replied, "Of course I do, dear. I'm wearing it to the rehearsal dinner the night before the wedding!"

NOW I ASK YOU – IS THERE A WOMAN OUT THERE, ANYWHERE, WHO WOULDN'T ENJOY THIS STORY?

SUBJECT: OH DEAR

Wee Willie was walking with Wanda, his new girlfriend, carrying her books home from grammar school. Both were eight years old. "Wanda," said Wee Willie with a worshipping gaze, "you are the first girl I have ever loved."

"Damn it!" said Wanda, "another beginner."

SUBJECT: DICTIONARY FOR DECODING PERSONAL ADS

Women's ads

40-ish	49
Adventurous	Slept with everyone.
Athletic	No Breasts.
Average Looking	Moooooooooooooooooo
Beautiful	Pathological Liar.
Emotionally Secure	On Medication.
Feminist	Fat
Friendship First	Reformed Bitch.
New Age	Body Hair In Wrong Places.
Open Minded	Desperate.
Outgoing	Loud and Embarrassing.
Professional	Bitch.
Voluptuous	Very Fat.
Large Frame	Hugely fat.
Wants Soul Mate	Stalker.

SUBJECT: DICTIONARY FOR DECODING PERSONAL ADS

Men's ads

40-ish	59
Adventurous	Slept with everything (including the neighbours dog and my ex wife's shower cap.
Athletic	I spend three hours a day in front of a mirror flexing my non biceps and twitching my boobs 'pecks' along to various Tom Jones tunes.
Average Looking	Danny Devito's body with Woody Allen's face.
Handsome	Personal add was written by mother.
Emotionally Secure	Still Married.
In favour of Women's rights	Pathological Liar.
Free Spirit	Open relationships wanted.
Friendship First	Small penis.
New Age	I'll try anything.
Old fashioned	Male chauvinist pig.
Open Minded	Any age/any sex.
Outgoing	I will talk/drink/shag anyone under the table.
Professional	Toff.
Cuddly	Beer belly.
Large Frame	Bed bound.
Wants Soul Mate	Middle aged virgin.

SUBJECT: DENTIST

A man goes into a dentistry and says, "You have to help me, I think I'm a Moth."

The Dentist says, "I think what you really need is a psychiatrist."

The man replies, "I knew that."

Dentist, "Then why did you come in here?"

Man, "The light was on."

SUBJECT: DONALD DUCK

Donald Duck and Daisy Duck were spending the night together in a hotel room and Donald wanted to have sex with Daisy. The first thing Daisy asked was, "Do you have a condom?"

Donald frowned and said, "No."

Daisy told Donald that if he didn't get a condom, they could not have sex. "Maybe they sell them at the front desk," she suggested. So Donald went down to the lobby and asked the hotel clerk if they had condoms.

"Yes, we do," the clerk said, and pulled one out from under the counter and gave it to Donald. The clerk asked, "Would you like me to put that on your bill?"

"No!" Donald quacked, "What kind of a friggin' pervert do you think I am?"

SUBJECT: DELTA, TWA AND UNITED

Tower: "Delta 351, you have traffic at ten o'clock, six miles!"
Delta 351: "Give us another hint! We have digital watches!"

Tower: "TWA 2341, for noise abatement turn right 45 Degrees."
TWA 2341: "Centre, we are at 35,000 feet. How much noise can we make up here?"
Tower: "Sir, have you ever heard the noise a 747 makes when it hits a 727?"

From an unknown aircraft waiting in a very long takeoff queue: "I'm f*cking bored!"
Ground Traffic Control: "Last aircraft transmitting, identify yourself immediately!"
Unknown aircraft: "I said I was f...ing bored, not f...ing stupid!"

O'Hare Approach Control to a 747: "United 329 heavy, your traffic is a Fokker, one o'clock, three miles, Eastbound."
United 329: "Approach, I've always wanted to say this... I've got the little Fokker in sight."

SUBJECT: DRIVING...

A man was driving down the road.

A woman is driving down the same road in the opposite direction.

As they pass each other, the woman leans out the window and yells, "pig!"

The man immediately leans out the window and yells, "cow!"

They each continue on their way, as the man rounds the next corner, he crashes into a huge pig in the middle of the road and dies.

If only men will listen.

SUBJECT: EVE'S SIDE OF THE STORY

After three weeks in the Garden of Eden, God came to visit Eve. "So, how is everything going?" inquired God.

"It is all so beautiful, God," she replied. "The sunrise and the sunset are breathtaking, the smells, the sights, everything is wonderful, but I have just one problem. It is these breasts you have given me. The middle one pushes the other two out and I am constantly knocking them with my arms, catching them on branches and snagging them on bushes. They are a real pain," reported Eve. And Eve went on to tell God that since many other parts of her body came in pairs, such as her limbs, eyes, ears, etc... she felt that having only two breasts might leave her body more "symmetrically balanced," as she put it.

"That is a fair point," replied God, "But it was my first shot at this, you know. I gave the animals six breasts, so I figured that you needed only half of those, but I see that you are right. I will fix it up right away."

And God reached down, removed the middle breast and tossed it into the bushes.

Three weeks passed and God once again visited Eve in the Garden of Eden. "Well, Eve how is my favourite creation?"

"Just fantastic," she replied, "But for one oversight on your part. You see, all the animals are paired off. The ewe has a ram and the cow has her bull. All the animals have a mate except me. I feel so alone."

God thought for a moment and said, "You know, Eve, you are right. How could I have overlooked this? You do need a mate and I will immediately create a man from a part of you. Now let's see... where did I put the useless boob?"

Now doesn't THAT make more sense than that crap about the rib?

SUBJECT: EXPEDITION

I have just been through the annual pilgrimage of torture and humiliation, known as buying a swimsuit. When I was a child in the 1950s the swim suit for a woman with a mature figure was designed for a woman with a mature figure, boned, trussed and reinforced, not so much sewn as engineered. They were built to hold back and uplift and they did a good job.

Today's stretch fabrics are designed for the pre-pubescent girl with a figure carved from a potato chip. The mature woman has a choice she can either front up at the maternity department and try on a floral suit with a skirt, coming away looking like a hippopotamus who escaped from Disney's Fantasia – or she can wander around the run-of-the-mill department store trying to make a sensible choice from what amounts to a designer range of fluorescent rubber bands. What choice is there?

I wandered around, made my choice and entered the chamber of horrors, known as the fitting room. The first thing I noticed was the extraordinary tensile strength of the material. The Lycra used in swim costumes was developed, I believe, by NASA to launch small rockets from a sling shot, which give the added bonus that if you manage to actually lever yourself into one, you are protected from shark attacks. The reason for this is that any shark taking a swipe at your passing midriff would immediately suffer whiplash.

I fought my way into the swimsuit, but as I twanged the shoulder strap in place, I gasped in horror… my bosom had disappeared! Eventually, I found one bosom cowering under my left armpit. It took a while to find the other. At last I located it flattened beside my seventh rib.

The problem is modern swimsuits have no bra cups. The mature woman is meant to wear her bosom spread across her chest like a speed bump. I realigned my speed bump and lurched toward the mirror to take a full view assessment. The swimsuit fitted alright, but unfortunately, it only fitted those bits of me willing to stay inside.

The rest of me oozed out rebelliously from top, bottom and sides. I looked like a lump of play dough wearing undersized cling wrap.

As I tried to work out where all those extra bits come from, the pre-pubescent sales girl popped her head through the curtains, "Oh there you are" she said admiring the swimsuit... I replied that I wasn't so sure, and asked what else she could show me. I tried on a cream crinkled one that made me look like a lump of masking tape, and a floral two piece which gave the appearance of an oversized napkin in a serviette ring.

I struggled into a pair of leopard skin bathers with ragged frill and come out looking like Tarzan's Jane pregnant with triplets and having a rough day.

I tried on a black number with a midriff and looked like a jellyfish in mourning.

I tried on a bright pink pair with such a high cut leg, I though I would have to wax my eyebrows to wear them.

Finally, I found a swimsuit that fitted... a two piece affair with shorts style bottom and a loose blouse-type top. It was cheap, comfortable, and bulge-friendly, So I bought it. My ridiculous search had a successful outcome.

When I got home, I found a label that said, "Material will become transparent in water."

SUBJECT: ENJOYING MORE ACCURATE COMPUTER RELATED ACRONYMS

PCMCIA   People Can't Memorise Computer Industry Acronyms

ISDN   It Still Does Nothing

APPLE   Arrogance Produces Profit-Losing Entity

SCSI   System Can't See It

DOS   Defunct Operating System

BASIC   Bill's Attempt to Seize Industry Control

IBM   I Blame Microsoft

DEC   Do Expect Cuts

CD-ROM   Consumer Device, Rendered Obsolete in Months

OS/2   Obsolete Soon, Too.

WWW   World Wide Wait

MACINTOSH   Most Applications Crash. If Not, The Operating System Hangs

LOTUS   Lots Of Trouble, Usually Serious.

SUBJECT: GLASS EYE

A man is dining in a fancy restaurant and there is a gorgeous redhead sitting at the next table. He has been checking her out since he sat down, but lacks the nerve to start a conversation.

Suddenly she sneezes, and her glass eye comes flying out of its socket towards the man.

He reflexively reaches out, grabs it out of the air, and hands it back.

"Oh my, I am so sorry," the woman says as she pops her eye back in place.

"Let me buy your dinner to make it up to you," she says.

They enjoy a wonderful dinner together, and afterwards they go to the theatre followed by drinks. They talk, they laugh, she shares her deepest dreams and he shares his. She listens.

After paying for everything, she asks him if he would like to come to her place for a nightcap... and stay for breakfast.

They have a wonderful, wonderful time.

The next morning, she cooks a gourmet meal with all the trimmings.

The guy is amazed!! Everything has been SO incredible!!!!

"You know," he said, "you are the perfect woman. Are you this nice to every guy you meet?"

"No," she replies..."

She says, "You just happened to catch my eye."

(Oh shut up, I just forward them, I don't write them)

SUBJECT: ELDERLY PATIENT

The pharmacist is going over the directions on the prescription bottle with the elderly patient. "Be sure not to take this more often than every four hours," says the pharmacist. "Don't worry," replied the patient. "It takes me four hours to get the lid off."

SUBJECT: THE EXPERT...

The efficiency expert concluded the lecture with a note of caution.

"You don't want to try these techniques at home."

"Why not" asked someone from the rear of the audience.

"I watched my wife's routine at breakfast for years" the expert explained. "She made lots of trips to the refrigerator, stove, table and cabinets, often carrying a single item at a time. "Hon" I suggested, "why don't you try to carrying several items at once?"

The voice at the back asked, "Did it save time?"

The expert replied, "Actually yes it used to take her 20 minutes to get breakfast ready."

"Now I do it in seven minutes."

SUBJECT: ENGLISH

Women's English

Yes	No.
No	Yes.
Maybe	No.
We Need	I want.
I am Sorry	You'll be sorry.
We need to talk	You're in trouble.
Sure, go ahead	You had better not.
Do what you want	You will pay for this later.
I am not upset	Of course, I am upset, you moron!
You're certainly at tentative tonight	Is sex all you ever think about.

Men's English

I am hungry	I am hungry.
I am sleepy	I am sleepy.
I am tired	I am tired.
Nice dress	Nice cleavage!
I love you	Lets have sex.
I am bored	Do you want to have sex.
May I have this dance	I'd like to have sex with you.
Can I tell you something	I'd like to have sex with you.
Do you want to go to a movie	I'd like to have sex with you.
Can I take you out to dinner	I'd like to have sex with you
I don't think those shoes go with that outfit	I'm gay.

SUBJECT: NEW ELEMENT DISCOVERED

Scientists Have Discovered a New Element

A major research institution has just announced the discovery of the heaviest element yet known to science. The new element has been named 'Governmentium'. Governmentium has one neutron, 12 assistant neutrons, 75 deputy neutrons, and 224 assistant deputy neutrons, giving it an atomic mass of 311. The 311 particles are held together by forces called morons, which are surrounded by vast quantities of lepton-like particles called persons. Since Governmentium has no electrons, it is inert. However, it can be detected, as it impedes every reaction with which it comes into contact.

A minute amount of Governmentium causes one reaction to take over four days to complete, when it would normally take less than a second.

Governmentium has a normal half-life of four years. It does not decay, but, instead undergoes a re-organization in which a portion of the assistant neutrons and deputy neutrons exchange places. In fact Governmentium mass will actually increase over time, since each reorganization will cause more morons to become neutrons, forming isodopes. This characteristic of the moron promotion leads scientists to believe Governmentium is formed whenever morons reach a certain quantity in concentration. This hypothetical quantity is referred to as 'Critical Morass'.

When catalysed with money Governmentium becomes Administratium, an element which radiates just as much energy, since it has half as many persons but twice as many morons.

SUBJECT: REASONS WHY THE ENGLISH LANGUAGE IS SO HARD TO LEARN

1. The bandage was wound around the wound.

2. The soldier decided to desert his dessert in the desert.

3. There was a row among the oarsmen about how to row.

4. The buck does funny things when the does are present.

5. To help with the planting, the farmer taught his sow to sow.

6. I had to subject the subject to a series of test.

7. The farm was used to produce produce.

8. The dump was so full, it had to refuse more refuse.

9. I did not object to the object.

10. The insurance was invalid for the invalid.

11. They were to close to the door to close it.

12. The wind was too strong to wind the sail.

13. Upon seeing the tear in the painting, I shed a tear.

14. Since there is no time like the present, he thought it was time to present the present.

15. We recite at a play and play at a recital, have noses that run and feet that smell, fill in a form by filling it out.

16. How can a slim chance and a fat chance be the same?

17. Did you know Boxing Rings are square?

18. How come your house burns down as it burns up, and alarm goes off when it goes on, when the stars are out, they are visible, but when the lights are out, they are invisible.

SUBJECT: A BIT OF FUN...

You can only pick one, so choose carefully!!
No cheating. Pick your dessert, and then look to see what this says about you!

If all of the desserts listed below were sitting in front of you,
Which would you choose? (Sorry, you can only pick one!)

Angel Food
Brownies
Lemon Meringue
Vanilla Cake/Chocolate Icing
Strawberry Short Cake
Chocolate Cake/Chocolate Icing
Ice Cream (your favourite flavour)
Carrot Cake

So think carefully what your choice will be!

OK – Now that you've made your choice, this is what research says about you!

Angel food – Sweet, loving, cuddly. You love all warm and fuzzy items. A little nutty at times. Sometimes you need an ice cream cone at the end of the day. Others perceive you as being childlike and immature at times.

Brownies – You are adventurous, love new ideas, are a champion of underdogs and a slayer of dragons. When tempers flare up, you bring out your sabre. You are always the odd ball with a unique sense of humour and direction. You tend to be very loyal.

Lemon Meringue – Smooth, sexy, and articulate with your hands, you are an excellent after dinner speaker and a good teacher.
But don't try to walk and chew gum at the same time. A bit of a diva at times, but you have a great many friends.

Vanilla Cake/Chocolate Icing – Fun loving, sassy, humorous. Not very grounded in life; very indecisive and lack motivation. Everyone enjoys being around you, but you are a practical joker. Others should be cautious in making you mad. However, you are a friend for life.

Strawberry Short Cake – Romantic, warm, loving. You care about other people and can be counted on in a pinch. You tend to melt. You can be overtly emotional and annoying at times.

Chocolate Cake/Chocolate Icing – Sexy, always ready to give and receive. Very creative, adventurous, ambitious, and passionate. You have a cold exterior but are warm on the inside. Not afraid to take chances. Will not settle for anything average in life. Love to laugh.

Ice Cream – You like sports, whether it be baseball, football, basketball, or soccer. If you could, you would like to participate, but you enjoy watching sports. You don't like to give up the remote control. You tend to be self centred and high maintenance.

Carrot Cake – You are a very fun loving person, who likes to laugh. You are fun to be with. People like to hang out with you. You are a very warm-hearted person and a little quirky at times. You have many loyal friends.

SUBJECT: FIRST PLACE

A couple has a dog that snores.

Annoyed because she can't sleep, the wife goes to the vet to see if he can help.

The vet tells the woman to tie a ribbon around the dog's testicles and he will stop snoring.

"Yeah right!" she says.

A few minutes after going to bed, the dog begins snoring, as usual. The wife tosses and turns, unable to sleep. Muttering to herself, she goes to the closet and grabs a piece of red ribbon and ties it carefully around the dog's testicles.

Sure enough, the dog stops snoring! The woman is amazed!

Later that night, her husband returns home drunk from being out drinking with his buddies. He climbs into bed, falls asleep and begins snoring loudly.

The woman thinks maybe the ribbon might work on him. So, she goes to the closet again, grabs a piece of blue ribbon and ties it around her husband's testicles.

Amazingly, it also works on him! The woman sleeps soundly. The husband wakes from his drunken stupor and stumbles into the bathroom. As he stands in front of the toilet, he glances in the mirror and sees a blue ribbon attached to his privates.

He is very confused, and as he walks back into the bedroom, he sees the red ribbon attached to his dog's testicles.

He shakes his head and looks at the dog and whispers, "I don't know where we were... or what we did... but, by God... We took first and second place."

SUBJECT: FATHER RAFFERTY

Mrs Donovan was walking down O'Connell Street in Dublin when she met up with Father Rafferty.

The Father said, "Top o' the mornin' to ye! Aren't ye Mrs Donovan and didn't I marry ye and yer husband two years ago?"

She replied, "Aye, that ye did, Father."

The Father asked, "And be there any wee ones yet?"

She replied, "No, not yet, Father."

The Father said, "Well now, I'm going to Rome next week, I'll light a candle for ye and yer husband."

She replied, "Oh, thank ye, Father."

They parted ways. Some years later they met again. The Father asked, "Well now, Mrs Donovan, how are ye these days?"

She replied, "Oh, very well, Father!"

The Father asked, "And tell me, have ye any wee ones yet?"

She replied, "Oh yes, Father! Three sets of twins and four singles, ten in all!"

The Father said, "That's wonderful! How is yer loving husband doing?"

She replied, "E's gone to Rome to blow out yer fookin' candle!"

SUBJECT: FIVE TIPS FOR A WOMAN...

1. It is important that a man helps you around the house and has a job.

2. It is important that a man makes you laugh.

3. It is important to find a man you can count on and doesn't lie to you.

4. It is important that a man loves you and spoils you.

5. It is important that these four men don't know each other.

SUBJECT: FACT

It used to be that only death and taxes were inevitable.
Now, of course, there's postage and handling, bank fees and petrol price rises.

SUBJECT: FOOT NOTE:

One saggy boob said to the other saggy boob:
"If we don't get some support soon, people will think we're nuts."

SUBJECT: FRENCH LESSON

Thought this might brighten up your day:

A French teacher was explaining to her class that in French, unlike English, nouns are designated as either masculine or feminine. House for instance is feminine 'La maison'. Pencil is masculine – 'Le Crayon'. A student asked, "What gender is computer?"

Instead of giving an answer, the teacher split the class into two groups, male and female and asked them to decide for themselves whether 'computer' should be masculine or feminine. Each group was asked to give four reasons for their recommendation.

The men's group decided that the computer should be feminine – 'la computer' because:

1. No one but their creator understands their internal logic.

2. The language they use to communicate with other computers is incomprehensible to everyone else.

3. Even the silliest mistakes are stored in long term memory for possible later retrieval.

4. As soon as you make a commitment to one, you find your self spending half your pay cheque on accessories for it.

The women's group however concluded that computers should be masculine – "le computer" because:

1. In order to do anything with them you have to turn them on.

2. They have a lot of data but still can't think for themselves.

3. They are supposed to help solve problems, but half the time they are the problem.

4. As soon as you commit to one you realise that if you had waited a little longer you could have got a better model.

SUBJECT: TRUE FACTS

Q: If you were to spell out numbers, how far would you have to go until you would find the letter 'A'?

A: One thousand.

Q: What do bullet proof vests, fire escapes, windshield wipers, and laser printers all have in common?

A: All invented by women.

Q: What is the only food that doesn't spoil?

A: Honey.

Q: Which day are there more collect calls than any other day of the year?

A: Father's Day.

SUBJECT: 20 WAYS TO SAY,
"YOUR FLY IS OPEN"

1. The cucumber has left the salad.

2. I can see the gun of Naverone.

3. Someone tore down the wall and Pink Floyd is hanging out.

4. You've got windows in your laptop.

5. Sailor Ned's trying to take a little shore leave.

6. Your soldier isn't so unknown now.

7. Quasimodo needs to go back in the tower and tend to his bell.

8. Paging Mr. Johnson. Paging Mr. Johnson.

9. You need to bring your tray table to the upright position.

10. Your pod bay door is open, Hal.

11. Elvis junior has left the building.

12. Mini Me is making a break for the escape pod.

13. Ensign Hayes is reporting a hull breach on the lower desk.

14. The Cruiser is not all the way in the garage.

15. Dr. Kimble has escaped.

16. You've got your fly set for 'Monica' instead of 'Hillary.'

17. Our next guest is someone who needs no introduction.

18. Cella door is open.

19. I'm talking about Shaft, can you dig it?

20. Always leaving the best till last, I thought you were crazy, now I see your nuts.

SUBJECT: FEMALE FRIENDSHIP VERSUS MALE MATESHIP

Friendship among women:
A woman doesn't come home at night. The next day she tells her husband that she slept over at a friend's house. The man calls his wife's ten best friends. None of them know about it.

Mateship among men:
A man doesn't come home at night. The next day he tells his wife that he slept over at a mate's house. The woman calls her husband's ten best mates. Eight of them say he did sleep over and two claim he's still there.

SUBJECT: THE FOLKS KNOW BEST

For three years, the young attorney had been taking his vacations at a country inn. The last time he'd finally managed an affair with the innkeeper's daughter.

Looking forward to an exciting few days, he dragged his suitcase up the stairs of the inn, then stopped short. There sat his lover with an infant on her lap.

"Helen, why didn't you write when you learned you were pregnant?" he cried. "I would have rushed up here, we could have gotten married, and the baby would have my name!"

"Well," she said, "when my folks found out about my condition, we sat up all night talkin' and talkin' and decided it would be better to have a bastard in the family than a lawyer."

SUBJECT: FRUIT CAKE RECIPE

1 cup water
1 cup sugar
4 large eggs
2 cups dried fruit
1 teaspoon baking soda
1 teaspoon salt
1 cup brown sugar
Lemon juice
Nuts
1 gallon whisky

Sample the whisky and check for quality. Take a large bowl.
Check the whisky again, to be sure it is of the highest quality.
Pour one level and drink. Repeat.
Turn the electric mixer on.
Beat one cup butter in a large, fluffy bowl.
Add one teaspoon sugar and beat again.
Make sure the whisky is still okay.
Try another cup.
Turn off the mixer.
Break two large eggs and add to the bowl and chuck in the cup and the dried fruit.
Mix on the turner.
If the fried druit gets stuck to the beaters, pry it loose with a drewscriver.
Sample the whisky to check the tonsisiticity.
Next, sift one cup of salt.
Or something. Who cares?
Check the whisky.
Now sift the lemon juice and strain the nuts.
Add one teaspoon of sugar or something.
Whatever, you can find.
Grease the oven.
Turn the cake tin to 350 degrees.
Don't forget to beat off the turner.
Throw the bowl out of the window.
Check the whisky again.
Go to bed.
Who the hell likes fruitcake anyway?

SUBJECT: GEOGRAPHY OF A WOMAN

Between eighteen and twenty a woman is like Africa, half discovered, half wild, naturally beautiful with fertile deltas.

Between twenty one and thirty a woman is like America, well developed and open to trade, especially for someone with cash.

Between thirty one and thirty five she is like India, very hot, relaxed and convinced of her own beauty.

Between thirty six and forty a woman is like France, gently aging but still warm and desirable place to visit.

Between forty one and fifty she is like Yugoslavia, lost the war, haunted by past mistakes. Massive reconstruction is now necessary.

Between fifty one and sixty she is like Russia, very wide and borders are not patrolled. The frigid climate keeps people away.

Between sixty one and seventy a woman is like Mongolia, with a glorious and all conquering past, but, alas, no future.

After seventy, she becomes Afghanistan. Almost every one knows where she is, but no one wants to go there.

SUBJECT: GATES OF HEAVEN

After a long illness a woman died and arrived at the gates of heaven.

While she was waiting for St. Peter to greet her she peeked through the gates and saw a beautiful banquet table. Sitting all around, in golden chairs, eating golden fruit, were her parents and all the other people she had loved and died before her.

They saw her and began calling out greetings, "Hello. How are you? We've been waiting for you. Welcome. Good to see you."
When St. Peter appeared the woman said to him, "This is such a beautiful place. How do I get in?"

"You have to spell a word," St. Peter told her. "Which word?" the woman asked.

"Love"

The woman was delighted. "L-O-V-E" she recited and St. Peter opened the Pearly Gates.

Six months later St. Peter came to the woman and asked her to watch the gates for him, for the day.

While she was guarding the gates of heaven, her husband arrived. "I'm surprised to see you," the woman said. "How have you been?" "Oh, I've been doing pretty well since you died," her husband told her. "I married the beautiful young nurse who took care of you when you were ill. Then I won the lottery. I sold our little house and bought a big mansion and my new wife and I travelled all around the world, flying fist class and staying in five star hotels."

"And what happened?"

"Well, I was water skiing today, in Hawaii, when I fell and the ski hit my head. So here I am. How do I get in?"

"You have to spell a word," the woman told him.

"Which word?" her husband asked.

"Czechoslovakia."

SUBJECT: GOT HIM GOOD...

Hubby was sitting at home watching football when his wife interrupts, "Honey, could you fix the light in the hallway? It's been flickering for weeks now."

He looks at her and says angrily, "Fix the light? Now? Does it look like I have an electrical logo printed on my forehead? I don't think so!"

"Well, could you fix the fridge door? I won't close properly."

"Fix the fridge door? Does it look like I have Westinghouse written on my forehead? I don't think so."

"Fine" she says. "Then could you at least fix the steps at the front door? They are about to break."

"Do I look like I have Mitre 10 written on my forehead? I don't think so. I've had enough of this , I'm going to the pub."

So hubby goes to the pub and drinks for a couple of hours. When he arrives home he notices the steps are fixed and the light is no longer flickering. He goes to the fridge to get a beer and notices the fridge door I also fixed.

"Honey, how'd this all get fixed?"

"Well," she says, "When you left I sat outside and cried. Just then a nice young man asked me what was wrong?" so I told him. He offered to do all the repairs and all I had to do was bake him a cake or have sex with him.

"So, what kind of cake did you bake him?" asks hubby.

She replied, "Hello! Do you see Sara Lee written on my forehead? I don't think so!"

SUBJECT: GOOD LISTENER

"A good listener is usually thinking about something else."
KIN HUBBARD

SUBJECT: SIR GALAHAD

King Arthur was in Merlin's laboratory where the great wizard was showing him his latest creation. It was a chastity belt, with a rather large hole in the most obvious place which made it basically useless.

"This is no good, Merlin!" the King exclaimed, "Look at this opening. How is this supposed to protect my lady, the Queen, when I'm on a long quest?"

"Ah, sire, just observe," said Merlin. He then selected his most worn out wand, one that he was going to discard anyway. He inserted it in the gaping aperture of the chastity belt whereupon a small guillotine blade came down and cut it neatly in two.

"Merlin, you are a genius!" said the grateful monarch. "Now I can leave, knowing that my Queen is fully protected."

After putting Guinevere in the device, King Arthur then set out upon a lengthy Quest.

Several years passed until he returned to Camelot. Immediately he assembled all of his knights in the courtyard and had them drop their trousers for an informal 'short arm' inspection. Sure enough, each and every one of them was either amputated or damaged in some way. All of them, except Sir Galahad.

"Sir Galahad," exclaimed King Arthur. "You are my one and only true knight! Only you among all the nobles have been true to me. What is it in my power to grant you? Name it and it is yours."

But, alas, Sir Galahad was speechless.

SUBJECT: GROWING OLD...

Reporters interviewing a 104-year-old woman, "And what do you think is the best thing about being 104?" the reporter asked. She simply replied, "No peer pressure."

The nice thing about being senile is you can hide your own Easter eggs.

Just before the funeral service, the undertaker came up to the very Elderly widow and asked, "How old was your husband?" "98," she replied. "Two years older than me." "So you're 96?" the undertaker commented. She responded, "Hardly worth going home, is it."

A 97-year-old man goes into his doctor's office and says, "Doc, I want my sex drive lowered." "Sir," replied the doctor, "you're 97-years-old! Don't you think your sex drive is all in your head?" "You're damned right it is!" replied the old man. "That's why I want it lowered!"

An elderly woman decided to prepare her will and told her preacher she had two final requests. First, she wanted to be cremated, and second, she wanted her ashes scattered over Wal-Mart! The preacher exclaimed, "Why Wal-Mart?". She replied, "Then I'll be sure my daughters will visit me twice a week."

My memory's not as sharp as it used to be.
Also, my memory's not as sharp as it used to be.

Know how to prevent sagging? Just eat till the wrinkles fill out.
I've still got it, but nobody wants to see it.

I'm getting into swing dancing. Not on purpose. Some parts of my body are just prone to swinging.

Don't think of it as getting hot flushes. Think of it as your Inner child playing with matches.

I don't think of it as hot flushes, they are my personal summers.

Don't let aging get you down. It's too hard to get back up.

Remember: You don't stop laughing because you grow old. You grow old because you stop laughing.

THE SENILITY PRAYER
Grant me the senility to forget the people I never liked anyway, the good fortune to run into the ones I do, and the eyesight to tell the difference.

Now, I think you're supposed to send this email on, but I can't remember...

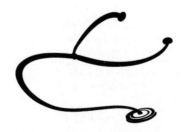

SUBJECT: ARE YOU GOOD OR BAD?

One day God was looking down at Earth and saw all of the rascally behaviour that was going on.

So he called one of His angels and sent the angel to Earth for a time.

When he returned, he told God, "Yes, it is bad on Earth; 95 per cent are misbehaving and only five per cent are not."

God thought for a moment and said, "Maybe I had better send down a second angel to get another opinion."

So God called another angel and sent him to Earth for a time too.

When the angel returned he went to God and said, "Yes, it's true. The Earth is in decline; 95 per cent are misbehaving, but five per cent are
being good."

God was not pleased. So, He decided to email the five per cent who were good, because He wanted to encourage them. Give them a little something to help them keep going.

Do you know what the email said?

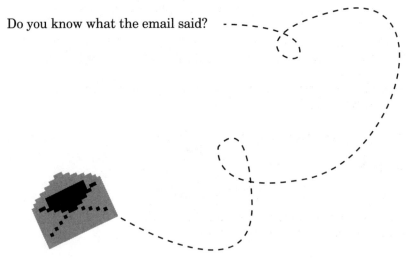

Okay, just wondering. I didn't get one either...

SUBJECT: GOD AND EVE

"God I have a problem"

"What is the problem Eve?"

"I know that you created me and provided this beautiful garden and all of these wonderful animals, as well as that hilarious comedic snake, but I'm just not happy."

"And why is that Eve?"

"God I am lonely and bored, and I'm sick the neck of apples."

"Well Eve, in that case, I have a solution, I shall create a man for you."

"Man? What is that God?"

"A flawed, base creature, with many bad traits. He'll lie, cheat and be vain. He will be witless and will revel in childish things. He'll be bigger than you and will like fighting hunting and killing things. He won't be smart, so he will need your advice to think properly. He will have a very limited emotional capacity and will need to be trained. He will look silly when aroused, but since you've been complaining, I'll create him in such a way that he will satisfy your physical needs. And most certainly will never be bored again!"

"Sounds great" says Eve, with ironically raised eyebrows, "But what is the catch, God."

"Well… you can have him on one condition."

"And what is that God?"

"As I said, he'll be proud arrogant and self admiring… so you'll have to let him believe I made him first. And it will have to be our little secret. You know, woman to woman."

SUBJECT: HEAVEN

This couple was 85 years old, and had been married for sixty years. Though they were far from rich, they managed to get by because they watched their pennies. And, though not young, they were both in very good health, largely due to the wife's insistence on healthy foods and exercise for the last three decades.

One day, their good health didn't help when they went on a rare vacation and their car crashed, sending them off to Heaven.

They reached the Pearly Gates, and St. Peter escorted them inside. He took them to a beautiful mansion, furnished in gold and fine silks, with a fully stocked kitchen and a waterfall in the master bath. A maid could be seen hanging their favourite clothes, freshly pressed, in the closet.

They gasped in astonishment when he said, "Welcome to Heaven. This will be your home now."

The old man asked Peter how much all this was going to cost.

"Why, nothing," Peter replied, "remember, this is your reward in Heaven."

The old man looked out the window and saw a championship golf course, finer and more beautiful than any ever built on Earth.

"What are the green fees?" grumbled the old man.

"This is heaven," St. Peter replied. "You can play for free, every day any starting time you wish."

Next they went to the clubhouse and saw the cuisine laid out before them, from seafood to steaks to exotic desserts, free flowing beverages and a fountain of champagne.

"Don't even ask," said St. Peter to the couple. "This is Heaven, it is all free for you to enjoy."

The old man looked around and glanced nervously at his wife.

"Well, where are the low fat and low cholesterol foods, and the decaffeinated tea?" he asked.

"That's the best part," St. Peter replied. "You can eat and drink as much as you like of whatever you like, and you will never get fat or sick. This is Heaven!"

The old man pushed, "No gym to work out at?"

"Not unless you want to," was the answer. "No testing my sugar or blood pressure or..."

"Never again. All you do here is enjoy yourself."

The old man glared at his wife and said, "You and your damn fat free muffins. We could have been here twenty years ago!"

SUBJECT: THE HUSBAND

My husband, not happy with my mood swings, bought me a mood ring the other day so her would be able to monitor my moods.

When I'm in a good mood the ring turns green.

When I'm in a bad mood it leaves a big red mark on his forehead.

Maybe nest time he'll buy me a diamond.

SUBJECT: MY HUSBAND

My husband came home today with a tube of KY jelly and said "This will make you happy tonight."

He was right. When he went out of the bedroom, I squirted it all over the doorknobs so he couldn't get back in.

SUBJECT: HA HA HA

Beau Bridges took a meteorology course in which the instructor was describing how hail is formed – much higher than the usual rain clouds. When he asked where specifically it happened, he was told, "Somewhere over the rain, Beau."
ALAN B. COMBS

What did the Marquis de Sade's wife say when asked why she was divorcing her husband?

Beats me!

SUBJECT: THE HARLEY MAN

The inventor of the Harley Davidson motorcycle, Arthur Davidson, died and went to heaven.

At the gates, St. Peter told Arthur, "Since you've been such a good man and your motorcycles have changed the world, as a reward you can be with anyone you want in Heaven." Arthur thought about it for a minute and then said, "I want to be with God." St. Peter took Arthur to the Throne Room and introduced him to God.

God recognized Arthur and commented, "Okay, so you were the one who invented the Harley Davidson motorcycle?"

Arthur said, "Yeah, that's me."

God commented, "Well, what's the big deal in inventing something that's pretty unstable, makes noise and pollution and can't run without a road?"

Arthur was apparently embarrassed, but finally spoke, "Excuse me, but aren't you the inventor of woman?"

God said, "Umm, yes."

"Well," said Arthur, "professional to professional, you have some major design flaws in your invention:
1. There's too much inconsistency in the front-end protrusion
2. It chatters constantly at high speeds
3. Most of the rear ends are too soft and wobble too much
4. The intake is placed way too close to the exhaust
5. And the maintenance costs are outrageous!!"

"Hmmmm, you may have some good points there," replied God, "Hold on."

God went to his Celestial super computer, typed in a few words and waited for the results. The computer printed out a slip of paper and God read it.

"Well, it may be true that my invention is flawed," God said to Arthur, "but according to these numbers, more men are riding my invention than yours."

SUBJECT: I HATE MY JOB

When you have an 'I Hate My Job' day, try the following:

On your way home from work, stop at your pharmacy and go to the thermometer section and purchase a rectal thermometer made by Johnson and Johnson. Be very sure you get this brand. When you get home, lock your doors, draw the curtains and disconnect the phone so you will not be disturbed.

Change into very comfortable clothing and sit in your favourite chair, open the package and remove the thermometer. Now, carefully place it on a table or a surface so that it will not become chipped or broken.

Now the fun part begins.

Take out the literature and read it carefully. You will notice that in small print there is a statement:

"Every rectal thermometer made by Johnson and Johnson is personally tested."

Now, close your eyes and repeat out loud five times, "I am so glad I do not work for quality control at Johnson and Johnson."

HAVE A NICE DAY AND REMEMBER, THERE IS ALWAYS SOMEONE ELSE WITH A JOB THAT IS WORSE THAN YOURS!!

HOME REMEDIES THAT REALLY WORK:

1. If you are choking on an ice cube, don't panic. Simply pour a cup of boiling water down your throat and presto! The blockage will be almost instantly removed.

2. Clumsy? Avoid cutting yourself while slicing vegetables by getting someone else to hold them while you chop away.

3. Avoid arguments with the Mrs about lifting the toilet by using the sink instead.

4. High blood pressure sufferers: simply cut yourself and bleed for awhile, thus reducing the pressure in your veins.

5. A mouse trap, placed on top of your alarm clock, will prevent you from rolling over and going back to sleep when you hit the snooze button.

6. If you have a bad cough, take a large dose of laxatives, then you will be afraid to cough.

7. Have a bad toothache? Hit your thumb with a hammer and then you will forget about the tooth ache.

AND... Sometimes we just need to remember what The Rules of Life really are:

You need only two tools:
WD-40 and duct tape.
If it doesn't move and it should, use WD-40.
If it moves and shouldn't, use the duct tape.

And finally... Be really good to your family and friends.
You never know when you are going to need them to hold the vegetables.

SUBJECT: HONK IF YOU LOVE JESUS...

The other day I went up to a local Christian bookstore and saw a honk if you love Jesus bumper sticker.

I was feeling particularly sassy that day because I had just come from a thrilling choir performance, followed by a thunderous prayer meeting, so I bought the sticker and put in on my bumper.

I was stopped at a red light at a busy intersection, just lost in thought about the Lord and how good He is and I didn't notice that the light had changed. It is a good thing someone else loves Jesus because if he hadn't honked, I'd never have noticed.

I found that LOTS of people love Jesus. Why, while I was sitting there, the guy behind started honking like crazy, and when he leaned out of his window and screamed, "For the love of God, GO! GO!"

What an exuberant cheerleader he was for Jesus. Everyone started honking! I just leaned out of my window and started waving and smiling at all these loving people. I even honked my horn a few times to share in the love.

There must have been a man from Florida back there because I heard him yelling something about a sunny beach...

I saw another guy waving in a funny way with only his middle finger stuck up in the air. When I asked my teenage grandson in the back seat what that meant, he said that it was probably a Hawaiian good luck sign or something.

Well, I've never met anyone from Hawaii, so I leaned out the window and gave him the good luck sign back. My grandson burst out laughing, why even he was enjoying this religious experience. A couple of the people were so caught up in the joy of the moment that they got out of their cars and started walking towards me.

I bet they wanted to pray or ask what church I attended, but this is when I noticed the light had changed. So, I waved to all my sisters and brothers grinning, and drove on through the intersection.

I noticed I was the only car that got through the intersection before the light changed again and I felt kind of sad that I had to leave them after all the love we had shared, so I slowed the car down, leaned out of the window and gave them all the Hawaiian good luck sign one last time as I drove away.

Praise the Lord for such wonderful folks!

SUBJECT: HOW THEY COME TO BE...

In Shakespeare's time, mattresses were secured on bed frames by ropes. When you pulled on the ropes the mattress tightened, making the bed firmer to sleep on. Hence the phrase...
"Good night, sleep tight."

It was the accepted practice in Babylon 4,000 years ago that for a month after the wedding, the bride's father would supply his son-in-law with all the mead he could drink. Mead is a honey beer and because their calendar was lunar based, this period was called the honey month, which we know today as the honeymoon.

SUBJECT: A MOMENT OF HUMOUR

A man goes to a party and has too much to drink.

His friends plead with him to let them take him home. He says no – he only lives a mile away.

About five blocks from party, the police pull him over for weaving ,and ask him to get out of the car and walk the line. Just as he starts, the police radio blares out a notice of a robbery taking place in a house just a block away. The police tell the party animal to stay put, they will be right back. They hop a fence and run down the street to the robbery.

The guy waits and waits and finally decides to drive home.

When he gets there, he tells his wife he is going to bed, and to tell anyone who might come looking for him that he has the flu and has been in bed all day. A few hours later the police knock on the door.

They ask if Mr. X is there and his wife says yes. They ask to see him and she replies that he is in bed with the flu and has been so all day.

The police have his driver's license. They ask to see his car and she asks why. They insist on seeing his car, so she takes them to the garage. She opens the door. There sitting in the garage is the police car, with all its lights still flashing

SUBJECT: HEAVEN...

I was shocked, confused, bewildered as I entered Heaven's door,
Not by the beauty of it all, by the lights or its decor.

But it was the folks in Heaven who made me sputter and gasp – the
thieves, the liars, the sinners, the alcoholics, the trash.

There stood the kid from seventh grade who swiped my lunch money
twice. Next to him was my old neighbour who never said anything
nice.

Herb, who I always thought was rotting away in hell, was sitting
pretty on cloud nine, looking incredibly well.

I nudged the angel, "What's the deal? I would love to hear Your take.
How'd all these sinners get up here? God must've made a mistake."

"And why's everyone so quiet, so somber? Give me a clue."

"Hush, child," said he. "They're all in shock. No one thought they'd
see you.

SUBJECT: THE INDIAN

A family was visiting an Indian reservation when they happen upon an old Indian laying face down in the middle of the road with his ear pressed firmly against the blacktop.

The father of the family asked the old tribesman what he was doing.

The tribesman began to speak haltingly. "A woman, late thirties, three kids, one barking dog in late model, four door station wagon, travelling at 65 miles per hour"

"That's amazing" exclaimed the father. "You can tell all of that by just listening to the ground?"

"No," said the old tribesman. "They just ran over me five minutes ago."

SUBJECT: "I AM"

'I am' is reportedly the shortest sentence in the English language.

Could it be that 'I do' is the longest sentence.

SUBJECT: ANOTHER INDIAN

There once was an Indian whose given name was Onestone, so named because he had only one testicle.

He hated that name and asked everyone to not to call him Onestone!

After years and years of torment, Onestone finally cracked and said, "If anyone calls me Onestone again I will kill them!"

The word got around and nobody called him that any more.
Then one day a young girl named Blue Bird forgot and said,
"Good morning, Onestone..."

He jumped up, grabbed her, and took her deep into the forest where he made love to her all day and all night. He made love to her all the next day, until Blue Bird died from exhaustion.

The word got around that Onestone meant serious business.

Years went by and no one dared call him by his given name until a woman named Yellow Bird returned to the village after being away for many years. Yellow Bird, who was Blue Bird's cousin, was overjoyed when she saw Onestone.

She hugged him and said, "Good to see you, Onestone..."

Onestone grabbed her, took her deep into the forest, then he screwed her all day, screwed her all night, screwed her all the next day, screwed her all the next night... but, Yellow Bird wouldn't die!

What is the moral of this story???

And the moral is...
You can't kill two birds with one stone!

SUBJECT: LITTLE JIMMY

For his birthday Little Jimmy asked for a mountain bike.

His father said, "Son, we'd love to give you one but the mortgage on this house is $400, 000 and your mother just lost her job. There's no way we can afford it right now."

The next day the father saw Little Jimmy heading out the front door with a suitcase. So he asked, "Son, where are you going?"

Little Jimmy told him, "I was walking past your room last night and I heard you tell Mum that you were pulling out. Then I heard her tell you to wait, because she was coming, too. And I'll be damned if I'm sticking around here by myself with a $400, 000 mortgage and no bike!"

SUBJECT: JOKE

What's the difference between a man and a supermarket trolley?

A supermarket trolley has a mind of its own

SUBJECT: JESUS AND SATAN

Jesus and Satan were having an ongoing argument about who was better at using the computer. They had been going at it for days, and God was tired of hearing all the bickering. Finally, God said, "Cool it. I am going to set up a test which will take two hours and it will judge who does the better job."

So Satan and Jesus sat down at the keyboards and typed away. They moused. They did spread sheets. They wrote reports. They sent faxes. They sent email. They sent out email with attachments. They downloaded. They did some genealogy reports. They made cards. They did every known job.

But, ten minutes before the time was up, lightning suddenly flashed across the sky, thunder rolled, the rain poured, and of course, the electricity went off. Satan stared at his blank screen and screamed every curse word known. Jesus just sighed.

The electricity finally flickered back on, and each of them restarted their computers. Satan started searching frantically screaming, "It's gone! It's all gone! I lost everything when the power went out!"

Meanwhile, Jesus quietly started printing out all his files from the past two hours. Satan observed this and became even more irate. "Wait! He cheated! How did he do it??!!"

God shrugged and said, "Jesus Saves."

SUBJECT: JOHN O'REILLY

A good Irish man, John O'Reilly, met regularly with the toastmasters club. One evening they were hitting the Guinness Stout and having a contest to see who could make the best toast.

John O'Reilly hoisted his beer and said, "Here's to spending the rest of me life between the legs of me wife!"

That won him the top prize for the best toast of the night!

He went home and told his wife, Mary, "I won the prize for the best toast of the night."

She said, "Aye, what was your toast?"

John said, "Here's to spending the rest of me life sitting in church beside me wife."

"Oh that is very nice indeed, John!" said Mary.

The next day, Mary ran into one of John's toasting buddies on the street corner. The man chuckled leeringly and said, "John won the prize last night, with a toast to you Mary."

She said, "Aye, and I was a bit surprised myself! You know, he's only been there twice! Once he fell asleep and the other time I had to pull him by the ears to make him come!"

SUBJECT: A JAZZ CHORD

Stevie Wonder is playing his first gig in Tokyo and the place is absolutely packed to the rafters. In a bid to break the ice with his new audience he asks if anyone would like him to play a request.

A little old Japanese man jumps out of his seat in the first row and shouts at the top of his voice, "Play a Jazz chord! Play a jazz chord!"

Amazed that this guy knows about the jazz influences in Stevie's varied career, the blind impresario starts to play an E minor scale and then goes into a difficult jazz melody for about ten minutes.

When he finishes the whole place goes wild. The little old man jumps up again and shouts, "No, no, play a Jazz chord, play a Jazz chord."

A bit peeved by this, Stevie, being the professional that he is, dives straight into a jazz improvisation with his band around the B flat minor chord and really tears the place apart.

The crowd goes wild with this impromptu show of his technical expertise.

The little old man jumps up again. "No, no. Play a Jazz chord, play a jazz chord."

Well and truly pissed off that this little guy doesn't seem to appreciate his playing ability. Stevie says to him from the stage "OK smart ass. You get up here and do it!"

The little old man climbs up onto the stage, takes hold of the mike And starts to sing...

"A jazz chord to say I ruv you..."

SUBJECT: BEST DEAR JOHN EVER

This is fabulous...

A Marine stationed in Afghanistan recently received a 'Dear John' letter from his girlfriend back home. It read as follows:

Dear Ricky,

I can no longer continue our relationship.
The distance between us is just too great. I must admit that I have cheated on you twice, since you've been gone, and it's not fair to either of us.
I'm sorry.
Please return the picture of me that I sent to you.

Love,
Becky

The Marine, with hurt feelings, asked his fellow Marines for any snapshots they could spare of their girlfriends, sisters, ex-girlfriends, aunts, cousins etc. In addition to the picture of Becky, Ricky included all the other pictures of the pretty gals he had collected from his buddies.

There were 57 photos in that envelope... along with this note:

Dear Becky,

I'm so sorry, but I can't quite remember who the hell you are.
Please take your picture from the pile, and send the rest back to me.

Take Care,
Ricky

Touché

SUBJECT: KIDS... GOT TO LOVE THEM

Slow down for three minutes to read this. It is so worth it. Touching words from the mouth of babes.

What does Love mean?

A group of professional people posed this question to a group of four to eight-year-olds, "What does love mean?" The answers they got were broader and deeper than anyone could have imagined.

"When my grandmother got arthritis, she couldn't bend over and paint her toenails any more. So my grandfather does it for her all the time, even when his hands got arthritis too. That's love."
REBECCA – age eight

"When someone loves you, the way they say your name is different. You just know that your name is safe in their mouth."
BILLY – age four

"Love is when a girl puts on perfume and a boy puts on shaving cologne and they go out and smell each other."
KARL – age five

"Love is when you go out to eat and give somebody most of your french fries without making them give you any of theirs."
CHRISSY – age six

"Love is what makes you smile when you're tired."
TERRI – age four

"Love is when my Mummy makes coffee for my Daddy and she takes a sip before giving it to him, to make sure the taste is OK."
DANNY – age seven

"Love is when you kiss all the time. Then when you get tired of kissing, you still want to be together and you talk more. My Mummy and Daddy are like that. They look gross when they kiss"
EMILY – age eight

"Love is what's in the room with you at Christmas if you stop opening presents and listen."
BOBBY – age seven

continued...

"If you want to learn to love better, you should start with a friend who you hate,"
NIKKA – age six

"Love is like a little old woman and a little old man who are still friends even after they know each other so well."
TOMMY – age six

"Love is when Mummy gives Daddy the best piece of chicken."
ELAINE – age five

"Love is when your puppy licks your face even after you left him alone all day."
MARY ANN – age four

"I know my older sister loves me because she gives me all her old clothes and has to go out and buy new ones."
LAUREN – age four

"When you love somebody, your eyelashes go up and down and little stars come out of you."
KAREN – age seven

"Love is when Mummy sees Daddy on the toilet and she doesn't think it's gross."
MARK – age six

"You really shouldn't say 'I love you' unless you mean it. But if you mean it, you should say it a lot. People forget."
JESSICA – age eight

And the final one – Author and lecturer Leo Buscaglia once talked about a contest he was asked to judge. The purpose of the contest was to find the most caring child. The winner was a four-year-old child whose next door neighbour was an elderly gentleman who had recently lost his wife.

Upon seeing the man cry, the little boy went into the old gentleman's yard, climbed onto his lap, and just sat there. When his Mother asked what he had said to the neighbour, the little boy said,

"Nothing, I just helped him cry"

SUBJECT: LOGO'S FOR T-SHIRTS

'I'm busy. You're Ugly. Have a nice day.'

Warning. I have an attitude, and know how to use it.

Remember my name, you'll be screaming it later.

Of course I don't look busy... I did it right the first time.

Why do people with closed minds always open their mouths.

I'm multi talented: I can talk and annoy you at the same time.

Do NOT start with me. You will NOT win.

You have the right to remain silent, so please shut up!

Don't press my buttons! I'm running out of places to hide the bodies.

Guys have feelings too. But like... who cares?

Next mood swing... six minutes.

I hate everybody and your next.

Please don't make me kill you.

And your point is...

All stressed out and no one to choke.

I'm one of those bad things that happen to good people.

Sorry, did I look interested...

SUBJECT: OLD LADIES

Two elderly ladies had been friends for many decades. Over the years they had shared all kinds of activities and adventures. Lately, their activities had been limited to meeting a few times a week to play cards.

One day they were playing cards when one looked at the other and said, "Now don't get mad at me. I know we've been friends for a long time... but I just can't think of your name! I've thought and thought, but I can't remember it. Please tell me what your name is."

Her friend glared at her. For at least three minutes she just stared and glared at her.

Finally she said, "How soon do you need to know?"

SUBJECT: LITTLE GIRL

A little girl walks into her parents bathroom and notices for the first time her fathers nakedness.

Immediately, she is curious: he has equipment that she doesn't. She asks, "What are those round things hanging there Daddy?"

Proudly, he replies, "Those sweetheart, are Gods apples of Life. Without them we wouldn't be here."

Puzzled, she seeks her Mummy out and tells her what Daddy had said. To which Mummy asks, "Did he say anything about the dead branch they're hanging from?"

SUBJECT: LIGHT RELIEF

Q: What do you call a handcuffed man.?
A: Trustworthy

Q: Why do female black widow spiders kill their males after mating?
A: To stop the snoring before it starts.

Q: How do you keep your husband from reading your email.?
A: Rename the mail folder "Instruction Manuals"

Q: What do you call an intelligent, good looking, sensitive man.?
A: A rumor.

Q: What does it mean when a man is in your bed gasping for breath and calling your name.?
A: You didn't hold the pillow down long enough.

Q: Why do men whistle when they are sitting on the toilet?
A: It helps them to remember which end they need to wipe.

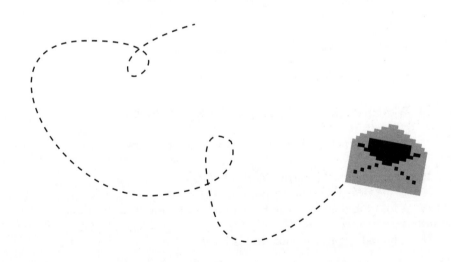

SUBJECT: FOR THOSE WHO ENJOY LANGUAGE (OR SEVERE DISTORTIONS, THEREOF)

1. A man's home is his castle, in a manor of speaking.

2. Dijon vu – the same mustard as before

3. Shotgun wedding: A case of wife or death.

4. A hangover is the wrath of grapes.

5. Does the name Pavlov ring a bell?

6. Reading while sunbathing makes you well red.

7. When two egotists meet, it's an I for an I.

8. A bicycle can't stand on its own because it is two tired.

9. Definition of a will: A dead give away.

10. Time flies like an arrow. Fruit flies like a banana.

11. She was engaged to a boyfriend with a wooden leg but broke it off.

12. A chicken crossing the road is poultry in motion.

13. If you don't pay your exorcist, you'll get repossessed.

14. When a clock is hungry, it goes back four seconds.

15. You feel stuck with your debt if you can't budge it.

16. Every calendar's days are numbered.

17. A lot of money is tainted – It taint yours and it taint mine.

18. A boiled egg in the morning is hard to beat.

19. A midget fortune-teller who escapes from prison is a small medium at large.

20. Those who get too big for their britches will be exposed in the end.

21. Once you've seen one shopping centre, you've seen a mall.

22. Bakers trade bread recipes on a knead-to-know basis.

23. Santa's helpers are subordinate clauses.

24. Acupuncture is a jab well done.

SUBJECT: THE AFTER LIFE...

An elderly couple made a deal that whoever died first would somehow come back to inform the other of the afterlife.

Their biggest fear was that there really was no heaven.

After a long life, the husband was the first to go and, true to his word, a few weeks later as his wife sat and watched TV, she heard a ghostly voice saying, "Maude... Maude..."

"Is that you, John?" she asked as she looked in vain around the room. The voice responded, "Yes Maude, I've come back just like we agreed."

"What's it like, John?" Maude asked.

John said, "Well, I get up in the morning and I have sex. Then I have breakfast, and after that more sex. I bathe in the sun for a while and then I have sex twice. I have lunch, then have sex pretty much all afternoon. After dinner I have sex until late at night and the next day it starts all over again."

"Oh, John," Maude said, "then surely you must be in heaven!"

"Not exactly," John said. "I'm a rabbit somewhere near Dubbo."

SUBJECT: LAWS OF LIFE

Murphy's First Law for Wives
If you ask your husband to pick up five items at the store and then you add one more as an afterthought, he will forget two of the first five.

Kauffman's Paradox of the Corporation
The less important you are to the corporation, the more your tardiness or absence is noticed.

The Salary Axiom
The pay raise is just large enough to increase your taxes and just small enough to have no effect on your take home pay.

Miller's Law of Insurance
Insurance covers everything except what happens.

First Law of Living
As soon as you start doing what you always wanted to be doing, you'll want to be doing something else.

Weiner's Law of Libraries
There are no answers, only cross references.

Isaac's Strange Rule of Staleness
Any food that starts out hard will soften when stale. Any food that starts out soft will harden when stale.

The Grocery Bag Law
The chocolate bar you planned to eat on the way home from the market is hidden at the bottom of the grocery bag.

Lampner's Law of Employment
When leaving work late, you will go unnoticed. When you leave work early, you will meet the boss in the parking lot.

SUBJECT: LIGHT RELIEF... OR MORE APTLY GROANERS

- Two antennas meet on a roof, fall in love and get married. The ceremony wasn't much, but the reception was excellent.

- Two hydrogen atoms walk into a bar. One says, "I've lost my electron." The other says, "Are you sure?" The first replies, "Yes, I'm positive..."

- A jumper cable walks into a bar. The bartender says, "I'll serve you, but don't start anything."

- Two peanuts walk into a bar, and one was a salted.

- A dyslexic man walks into a bra.

- A man walks into a bar with a slab of asphalt under his arm and says, "A beer please, and one for the road."

- Two cannibals are eating a clown. One says to the other, "Does this taste funny to you?"

- "Doc, I can't stop singing *The Green, Green Grass of Home*." "That sounds like Tom Jones Syndrome." "Is it common?" "*It's Not Unusual.*"

- Two cows standing next to each other in a field, Daisy says to Dolly, "I was artificially inseminated this morning." "I don't believe you," said Dolly. "It's true, no bull!" exclaimed Daisy.

- An invisible man marries an invisible woman. The kids were nothing to look at either.

- Deja Moo: The feeling that you've heard this bull before.

- A man takes his Rottweiler to the vet and says, "My dog's cross-eyed, is there anything you can do for him?" "Well," says the vet, "let's have a look at him." So he picks the dog up and examines his eyes, then checks his teeth. Finally, he says, "I'm going to have to put him down." "What? Because he's cross-eyed?" "No, because he's really heavy."

SUBJECT: THE MAMMOGRAM...

Many women are afraid of their first mammogram, but there's no need to worry. By taking a few minutes each day for a week preceding the exam, and doing the following practice exercises, you will be totally prepared.

And you can do this right in your own home!

Exercise One
Open your refrigerator door and insert one breast between the door and the main box. Have one of your strongest friends slam the door shut and lean on the door for good measure. Hold that position for five seconds (while you hold your breath). Repeat again, in case the first time wasn't effective enough.

Exercise Two
Visit your garage at 3 a.m. when the temperature of the cement floor is just perfect. Take off your clothes and lie comfortably on the floor with one breast wedged under the rear tire of the car. Ask a friend to slowly back the car up until your breast is sufficiently flattened and chilled. Turn over and repeat for the other breast.

Exercise Three
Freeze two metal book ends overnight. Strip to the waist. Invite a stranger into the room. Press the book ends against one of your breasts. Smash the book ends together as hard as you can. Set an appointment with the stranger to meet next week and do it again!!

CONGRATULATIONS!
Now you have nothing at all to worry about when you go for you Mammogram!

SUBJECT: ARE YOU A MEAN MUM?

Someday when my children are old enough to understand the Logic that motivates a parent, I will tell them, as my Mean Mum told me: I loved you enough... to ask where you were going, with whom, and what time you would be home.

I loved you enough to be silent and let you discover that your new best friend was a creep.

I loved you enough to stand over you for two hours while you cleaned your room, a job that should have taken 15 minutes.

I loved you enough to let you see anger, disappointment, and tears in my eyes.

Children must learn that their parents aren't perfect.

I loved you enough to let you assume the responsibility for your actions even when the penalties were so Harsh they almost broke my heart.

But most of all, I loved you enough to say NO when I knew you would hate me for it.

Those were the most difficult battles of all.
I'm glad I won them, because in the end you won, too. And someday when your children are old enough to understand the logic that motivates parents, you will tell them.

Was your Mum mean? I know mine was. We had the meanest mother In the whole world! While other kids ate candy for breakfast, we had to have cereal, eggs, and toast. When others had a Pepsi and a Twinkie for lunch, we had to eat sandwiches. And you can guess our mother fixed us a dinner that was different from what other kids had, too. Mother insisted on knowing where we were at all times. You'd think we were convicts in a prison.

She had to know who our friends were, and what we were doing with them. She insisted that if we said we would be gone for an hour, we would be gone for an hour or less. We were ashamed to admit it, But she had the nerve to break the Child Labour Laws by making us work. We had to wash the dishes, make the beds, learn to cook, vacuum the floor, do laundry, empty the trash and all sorts of cruel jobs.

I think she would lie awake at night thinking of more things for us to do.

She always insisted on us telling the truth, the whole truth, and nothing but the truth.

By the time we were teenagers, she could read our minds and had eyes in the back of her head.

Then, life was really tough!

Mother wouldn't let our friend's just honk the horn when they drove up.

They had to come up to the door so she could meet them. While everyone else could date when they were 12 or 13, we had to wait until we were 16.

Because of our mother we missed out on lots of things other kids experienced.

None of us have ever been caught shoplifting, vandalizing other's property or ever arrested for any crime.

It was all her fault.

Now that we have left home, we are all educated, honest adults. We are doing our best to be mean parents just like Mum was.

I think that is what's wrong with the world today. It just doesn't have enough Mean Mums!

SUBJECT: MY FIRST TIME...

The sky was dark, the moon was high.
We were together, just she and I.
Her hair was brown, her eyes were blue.
I knew just what she wanted to do.

So with my hand I did my best.
I ran my hand over her breast.
Her body was good, her hair was fine.
I ran my hand down her spine.

I felt a shock, I felt her heart.
Slowly she spread her legs apart.
I knew she was ready, but I didn't know how.
This was the first time, milking a cow.

SUBJECT: AS I MATURE...

I've learned that you cannot make someone love you. All you can do is stalk them and hope they panic and give in.

I've learned that no matter how much I care, some people are just assholes.

I've learned that it takes years to build up trust, and it only takes suspicion, not proof, to destroy it.

I've learned that you can get by on charm for about fifteen minutes. After that, you'd better have a big willy or huge boobs.

I've learned that you shouldn't compare yourself to others – they are more screwed up than you think.

I've learned that you can keep vomiting long after you think you're finished.

I've learned that we are responsible for what we do, unless we are celebrities.

I've learned that regardless of how hot and steamy a relationship is at first, the passion fades, and there had better be a lot of money to take its place!

I've learned that 99 per cent of the time when something isn't working in your house, one of your kids did it.

I've learned that the people you care most about in life are taken from you too soon and all the less important ones just never go away.

Pass this along to some of your friends, something good might happen... if not tough shit.

SUBJECT: MARRIAGE - ENJOY...

Marriage – Part I
A typical macho man married typical good looking lady and after the wedding, he laid down the following rules:

1. "I'll be home when I want, if I want and at the time I want and I don't expect any hassle from you.
2. I expect a great dinner to be on the table unless I tell you that I won't be home for dinner.
3. I'll go hunting, fishing, drinking and card playing when I want with my buddies and don't you ever complain about it. Those are my rules. Any comments?

His new bride replied, "No, that's all just fine with me. But please understand that there will be sex here at seven o'clock every night whether you're here or not."

(DAMN SHE'S GOOD!)

Marriage – Part II
Husband and wife had a bitter quarrel on the day of their 40th wedding anniversary! The husband yells, "When you die, I'm getting you a headstone that reads, 'Here Lies My Wife – Cold As Ever'"

"Yeah?" she replies. "When you die, I'm getting you a headstone that reads, 'Here Lies My Husband Stiff At Last'"

(HE ASKED FOR IT!)

Marriage – Part III
Husband (a doctor) and his wife are having a fight at the breakfast table.

Husband gets up in a rage and says, "And you are no good in bed either," and storms out of the house. After sometime, he realizes he was nasty and decides to make amends and rings her up.

She comes to the phone after many rings, and the irritated husband says, "what took you so long to answer the phone?"

She says, "I was in bed."

"In bed this early, doing what?"
"Getting a second opinion!"

(YEP, HE HAD THAT ONE COMING, TOO!)

Marriage – Part IV

A man has six children and is very proud of his achievement. He is
so proud of himself, that he starts calling his wife, "Mother of Six" in
spite of her objections.
One night, they go to a party. The man decides that it's time to go
home and wants to find out if his wife is ready to leave as well.
He shouts at the top of his voice, "Shall we go home 'Mother of
Six?' His wife, irritated by her husband's lack of discretion, shouts
back, "Any time you're ready, Father of Four."

(RIGHT ON, LADY!)

Marriage – Part V – The Silent Treatment

A man and his wife were having some problems at home and were
giving each other the silent treatment. Suddenly, the man realised
that the next day, he would need his wife to wake him at 5 a.m. for
an early morning business flight.

Not wanting to be the first to break the silence (and LOSE), he wrote
on a piece of paper, "Please wake me at 5 a.m."
He left it where he knew she would find it.

The next morning, the man woke up, only to discover it was 9 a.m.
and he had missed his flight.

Furious, he was about to go and see why his wife hadn't wakened
him, when he noticed a piece of paper by the bed. The paper said,
"It is 5 a.m. Wake up."

God may have created man before woman, but there is always a
rough draft before the masterpiece.

SUBJECT: THE ALMOST MILLIONAIRE

When John found out he was going to inherit a fortune when his sickly father died, he decided he needed a woman to enjoy it with.

So one evening he went to a singles bar where he spotted the most beautiful woman he had ever seen. Her natural beauty took his breath away.

"I may look like just an ordinary man," he said as he walked up to her, "but in just a week or two, my father will die, and I'll inherit 20 million dollars."

Impressed, the woman went home with him that evening and, three days later, she became his stepmother.

Women can be so much smarter than men...

SUBJECT: MMM

Some of the things that we consider ponderable –

1. Should crematoriums give discounts for burn victims?

2. Whose cruel idea was it to put a 'S' in the word Lisp?

3. If someone with multiple personalities threatens suicide is it considered a hostage situation?

4. If a man with no arms has a gun, is he armed?

5. When cheese gets its picture taken, what does it say?

6. Why are a wise man and wise guy opposites?

7. Why do overlook and oversee mean opposite things?

8. What should you do if you see an endangered animal eating an endangered plant?

9. Isn't it scary that doctors call what they do a 'practice'?

10. Where do forest rangers go to get away from it all?

11. Why isn't 11 pronounced onety-one?

12. Why do they use sterilised needles for lethal injections?

13. Why did kamikaze pilots wear helmets?

14. What WAS the best thing BEFORE sliced bread?

15. Why is it that if someone tells you that there are 1 billion stars in the universe you will believe them, but if they tell you a wall has wet paint you will have to touch it to be sure?

16. If people from Poland are called, 'Poles', why aren't people from Holland called 'Holes'?

17. If a pig loses its voice, is it disgruntled?

SUBJECT: MINI COOPER

This guy went to work without realising he did not zip his trousers.

His secretary noticed and said to him, "You didn't close the garage."

The guy did not understand so he went to call his wife and asked if the garage door was closed. His wife said, "of course honey, the garage door is closed."

The guy went to his secretary and told her that his wife said the garage door was closed. The lady realised that he did not understand her, so she moved a little closer and said, "I mean you did not zip your trousers." The guy said, "OK," and went to his office and zipped his trousers.

When he came back he said to his secretary, "When the garage was open, did you see my Mercedes Benz?"

The lady said, "No, only a Mini Cooper with two flat tyres"

SUBJECT: MANAGEMENT VERSUS IT

A man in a hot air balloon was lost. He reduced his altitude and spotted a woman below.

He descended a bit more and shouted, "Excuse me, can you help? I don't know where I am. I promised to meet a colleague and now I'm late."

The woman below replied, "You're in a hot air balloon hovering approximately ten metres above the ground. You're position is about 34 degrees south latitude and 150 degrees east longitude."

"That's impressive, you must be in I.T." said the balloonist. "I am," replied the woman, "how did you know?"

"Well," he answered, "everything you told me is technically correct, but I've no idea what to make of your information, and the fact is I'm still lost. Frankly, you've been of little help. If anything, you've delayed my trip."

The woman below responded, "You have to be in Senior Management."

"I am!" replied the balloonist, "..but how did you know?"

"Easy," said the woman. "You don't know where you are, or where you're going. You have risen to where you are, due to a lot of hot air. You made a promise, which you've no idea how to keep. You expect those beneath you to solve your problem. The fact is, you are in exactly the same position you were in before we met, but now, somehow, it's my fault."

SUBJECT: MARRIAGE

At a cocktail party, one woman said to another,
"Aren't you wearing your wedding ring on the wrong finger?"
"Yes, I am. I married the wrong man."

You have two choices in life:
You can stay single and be miserable,
or get married and wish you were dead.

If you want your spouse to listen and pay strict attention to every word you say – talk in your sleep.

A lady inserted an ad in the classifieds:

"Husband Wanted."
Next day she received a hundred letters.
They all said the same thing:
"You can have mine."

SUBJECT: MEN NEVER LISTEN

On a flight to Chicago, a gentleman had made several attempts to get into the men's bathroom, but it had always been occupied.

The flight attendant noticed his predicament. "Sir", she said, "you may use the ladies room if you promise not to touch any of the buttons on the wall."

He did what he needed to, and as he sat there he noticed the buttons he had promised not to touch. Each button was identified by letters: WW, WA, PP, and a red one labelled ATR. Who would know if he touched them?

He couldn't resist, he pushed WW. Warm water was sprayed gently upon his bottom. What a nice feeling, he thought. Men's bathrooms don't have nice things like this.

Anticipating greater pleasure, he pushed the WA button.

Warm air replaced the warm water, gently drying his underside. When this stopped, he pushed the PP button. A large powder puff caressed his bottom adding a fragile scent of spring flowers to this unbelievable pleasure. The ladies bathroom was more than a bathroom, it is tender loving pleasure.

When the powder puff completed its pleasure, he couldn't wait to push the ATR button which he knew would be supreme ecstasy.

Next thing he knew he was in a hospital as soon as he opened his eyes. A nurse was staring down at him with a smirk on her face.

"What happened?" he exclaimed.

"You pushed one too many buttons," replied the nurse.

"The last button marked ATR was an Automatic Tampon Remover. Your penis is under your pillow."

SUBJECT: THE MOTHER-IN-LAW

A young lady came home from her date, rather sad.

She told her mother, "Jeff proposed to me an hour ago."

"Then why are you so sad?" her mother asked.

"Because he also told me he was an atheist. Mum he doesn't even believe in hell."

"Marry him anyway. Between the two of us, we'll show him how wrong he is."

SUBJECT: MUM TAUGHT ME...

My Mum taught me to appreciate a job well done.
"If you're going to kill each other, do it outside.
I just finished cleaning."

My Mum taught me religion.
"You better pray that will come out of the carpet."

My Mum taught me about time travel.
"If you don't clean up this room, I'm going to knock you into the
middle of next week."

My Mum taught me logic.
"Because I said so, that's why."

My Mum taught me foresight.
"Make sure you wear clean underwear in case you're
involved in an accident.

My Mum taught me irony.
"Keep crying and I'll give you something to cry about."

My Mum taught me the science of osmosis.
"Shut your mouth and eat your dinner!"

My Mum taught me contortionism.
"Will you look at the dirt on the back of your neck!"

My Mum taught me stamina.
"You'll sit there until all the vegetables are finished."

My Mum taught me weather.
"It looks as if a cyclone came through here."

My Mum taught me how to solve physics problems.
"If I yelled because I saw a meteor coming toward you,
would you listen then?"

My Mum taught me hypocrisy.
"If I've told you once, I've told you a thousand times. Don't
exaggerate."

SUBJECT: "ARE YOU THE MANAGER?"

A very attractive lady goes up to a bar in a quiet rural pub. She gestures alluringly to the bartender who comes over immediately. When he arrives, she seductively signals that he should bring his face closer to hers.

When he does she begins to gently caress his full beard. "Are you the manager?" she asks, softly stroking his face with both hands.

"Actually, no," the man replied.

"Can you get him for me? I need to speak to him" she says, running her hands beyond his beard and into his hair.

"I'm afraid I can't," breathes the bartender.

"Is there anything I can do?"

"Yes, there is. I need you to give him a message," she continues running her forefinger across the bartender's lips and slyly popping a couple of her fingers into his mouth and allowing him to suck them gently.

"What should I tell him?" the bartender manages to say.

"Tell him," she whispers, "there is no toilet paper, hand soap, or paper towels in the ladies room."

SUBJECT: MEN JOKES

Q: Why do men become smarter during sex?
A: Because they are plugged into a genius

Q: Why don't men blink during sex?
A: They don't have enough time.

Q: Why does it take 1 million sperm to fertilise one egg?
A: They don't stop to ask directions .

Q: Why do men snore when they lie on their backs?
A: Because their balls fall over their butt hole and they vapour lock.

Q: Why were men given larger brains than dogs?
A: So they won't hump women's legs at cocktails parties.

Q: Why did God make men before women?
A: You need a rough draft before you make a final copy.

Q: How many men does it take to put a toilet seat down?
A: Don't know! It never happened.

And my personal favourite:

Q: Why did God put men on Earth?
A: Because a vibrator can't mow the lawn

Remember, if you haven't got a smile on your face and laughter in your heart... Then you are just an old sour fart.

SUBJECT: MIDDLE WIFE

I've been teaching now for about fifteen years. I have two kids myself, but the best birth story I know is the one I saw in my own second grade classroom a few years back.

When I was a kid, I loved show-and-tell. So I always have a few sessions with my students. It helps them get over shyness and usually, show-and-tell is pretty tame. Kids bring in pet turtles, model aeroplanes, pictures of fish they catch, stuff like that. And I never, ever place any boundaries or limitations on them. If they want to lug it in to school and talk about it, they're welcome.

Well, one day this little girl, Erica, a very bright, very outgoing kid, takes her turn and waddles up to the front of the class with a pillow stuffed under her sweater. She holds up a snapshot of an infant. "This is Luke, my baby brother, and I'm going to tell you about his birthday."

"First, Mum and Dad made him as a symbol of their love, and then Dad put a seed in my Mum's stomach, and Luke grew in there. He ate for nine months through an umbrella cord."

She's standing there with her hands on the pillow, and I'm trying not to laugh and wishing I had my camcorder with me. The kids are watching her in amazement.

"Then, about two Saturdays ago, my Mum starts saying and going, 'Oh, oh, oh, oh!' "Erica puts a hand behind her back and groans. "She walked around the house for, like an hour, 'Oh, oh, oh!'" Now this kid is doing a hysterical duck walk and groaning. "My Dad called the middle wife. She delivers babies, but she doesn't have a sign on the car like the Domino's man. They got my Mum to lie down in bed like this."

Then Erica lies down with her back against the wall. "And then, pop! My Mum had this bag of water she kept in there in case he got thirsty, and it just blew up and spilled all over the bed, like psshhheew!" This kid has her legs spread and with her little hands are miming water flowing away. It was too much! "Then the middle wife starts saying 'push, push,' and 'breathe, breathe.' They started counting, but never even got past ten. Then, all of a sudden, out comes my brother. He was covered in yucky stuff, they all said it was from Mum's play centre! So there must be a lot of stuff inside there."

Then Erica stood up, took a big theatrical bow and returned to her seat. I'm sure I applauded the loudest. Ever since then, if it's show-and-tell day, I bring my camcorder, just in case another Erica comes along.

SUBJECT: MENTALITY

Jim and Edna were both patients in a mental hospital.

One day while they were walking past the hospital swimming pool, Jim suddenly jumped into the deep end. He sank to the bottom of the pool and stayed there. Edna promptly jumped in to save him. She swam to the bottom and pulled Jim out.

When the director of Nursing became aware of Edna's heroic act, she considered her to be mentally stable.

When she went to tell Edna the news she said, "Edna, I have good news and bad news. The good news is you're being discharged since you were able to rationally respond to a crisis by jumping in and saving the life of another patient! I have concluded that your act displays sound mindedness. The bad news is that Jim, the patient you saved, hung himself in his bathroom with the belt to his robe right after you saved him. I am sorry, but he's dead.

Edna replied, "He didn't hang himself, I put him there to dry. How soon can I go home?"

SUBJECT: MEN ARE LIKE...

PLACE MATS
They only show up when there is food on the table.

MASCARA
They usually run at the first sign of emotion.

BIKE HELMETS
They're good in emergencies, but usually just look silly.

GOVERNMENT BONDS
They take so long to mature.

COPIERS
You need them in reproduction, but that's about it.

LAVA LAMPS
Fun to look at, but not that bright.

BANK ACCOUNTS
Without a lot of money, they don't generate a lot of interest.

HIGH HEELS
They're easy to walk on, once you get the hang of it.

CURLING IRONS
They're always hot, and always in your hair.

MINI SKIRTS
If you're not careful, they'll creep up your legs.

HAND GUNS
Keep one around long enough and you're gonna want to use it.

SUBJECT: NEIGHBOURS

Three women were chatting over mid morning coffee and complaining about the weather.

"It's hopeless," said Mrs Jones said. "More often than not, I put my washing out and 15 minutes starts to rain."

"I agree," said Mrs Smith. "This morning when I put out my washing, the sun was shining. Now look at it!"

Mrs Jones and Mrs Smith looked over at Mrs Flynn, who at this point had not said a word.

"Now I come to think about it Mrs Flynn, your always lucky when you put your washing out. What's the secret?" they asked.

"Well it's quite simple," replied Mrs Flynn. "When I wake up in the morning I look at my husband and if his penis is hanging to the left then I know it is going to rain. If it's hanging to the right, then I know it is going to be bright and sunny day."

"Ah ha," said Mrs Jones, "But what if he has an erection?"

"Well on a day like that I don't do any laundry..."

SUBJECT: NEW PRODUCT

Announcing the new Built-in Orderly Organized Knowledge device, otherwise known as a Book.

It's a revolutionary breakthrough in technology: no wires, no electric circuits, no batteries, nothing to be connected or switched on. It's so easy to use even a child can operate it. Just lift the cover. Compact and portable, it can be used anywhere... even sitting in an armchair by the fire... yet it is powerful enough to hold as much information as a CD ROM Disk.

Here's how it works: each BOOK is constructed of sequentially numbered sheets of paper (recyclable), each capable of holding thousands of bits of information. These pages are locked together with custom-fit device called a binder which keeps the sheets in their correct sequence. By using both sides of each sheet, manufacturers are able to cut the cost in half.

Each sheet is scanned optically, registering information directly to the brain. A flick of the finger takes you to the nest sheet. The BOOK may be taken up at any time and used by merely opening it. The 'Browse' feature allows you to move instantly to any sheet, and move forward or backwards as you wish. Most come with an 'Index' feature, which pinpoints the exact location of any selected information for instant retrieval.

An optional 'BOOKmark' accessory allows you to open the BOOK to the exact place you left it in at a previous session... even if the BOOK has been closed. BOOKmarks fit universal designs standards: thus a single BOOKmark can be used in BOOKs by various manufactures.

Portable, durable and affordable, the BOOK is the entertainment wave of the future, and many new titles are expected soon, due to the surge in popularity of its programming tool, the Portable Erasable-Nib Cryptic Intercommunication Language stylus (PENCIL)

SUBJECT: NORMAL

It doesn't hurt to take a hard look at yourself from time to time, and this should help get you started.

During a visit to the mental asylum, a visitor asked the Director what the criteria was which defined whether or not a patient should be institutionalised.

Well, said the Director, "we will fill up a bathtub, and then we offer a teaspoon, a teacup and a bucket to the patient and ask him or her to empty the bathtub."

"Oh, I understand," said the visitor. "A normal person would use the bucket because it's bigger than the spoon or the teacup."

"No," said the Director, "A normal person would pull the plug."

Do you want a room with or without a view?

SUBJECT: NAUGHTY

Three men go to a brothel and are told the payment value is three times the size of their penis.

When they left one complained of paying $38, the second of paying $30.

The third paid $6.

He paid on the way out.

SUBJECT: OH DEAR...

Following a night out with a few friends, a man brought them back to show off his new flat. After the grand tour, the visitors were rather perplexed by the large gong taking pride of place in the lounge.

"What's that big brass gong for?" one of the guests asked.

"Why, that's my Speaking Clock," the man replied.

"How does it work?"

"I'll show you," the man said, giving the gong an ear shattering blow with an unpadded hammer.

Suddenly, a voice from the other side of the wall screamed,

"For God's sake, you bastards, it's twenty to two in the bloody morning!!"

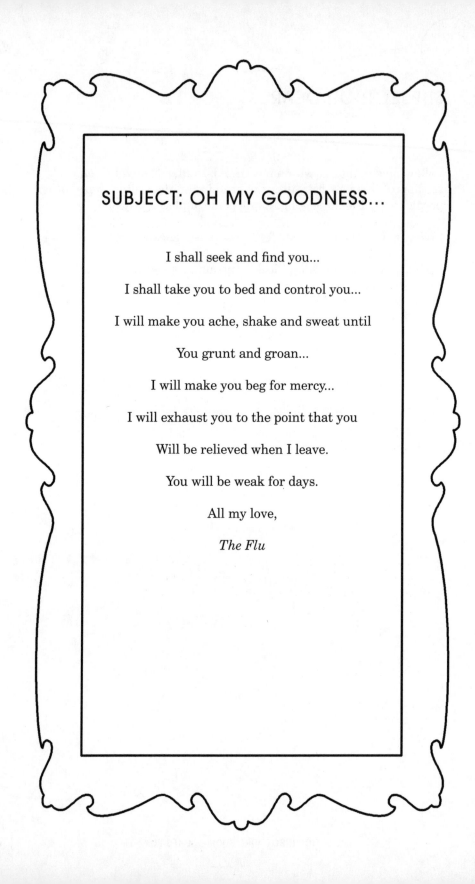

SUBJECT: OH MY GOODNESS...

I shall seek and find you...

I shall take you to bed and control you...

I will make you ache, shake and sweat until

You grunt and groan...

I will make you beg for mercy...

I will exhaust you to the point that you

Will be relieved when I leave.

You will be weak for days.

All my love,

The Flu

SUBJECT: ONE SAD TALE

I Will Survive... SING IT GIRLS!!!

At first I was afraid, I was petrified.
When you said you had ten inches, Lord I almost died!
But I'd spent so many years just waiting for a man that long,
That I grew strong, and I knew that I could take you on...
But there you are, another lie,
I was ready for a Big Mac and you've brought me a french fry!
I should have known that it was bullshit, just a sad pathetic dream
Should have known there was no Anaconda lurking in those jeans!

Go on now – go, ! Walk out the door,
Don't you promise me ten inches, then turn up with only four!
Weren't you a brat to think I wouldn't find you out!?
Don't you know we're only joking when we say size don't count??!!

[Chorus]

I will survive! I will survive!
Cuz as long as I have batteries,
My sex life's gonna thrive!
I will always have good sex,
with a handful of latex!
I will survive! I will survive! Hey! Hey!

It took all my self control not to laugh out loud,
When I saw your little weiner standing tall and proud!
But to hell with your ego and to hell with all your needs,
Now I'm saving all my lovin' for a cordless multi speed!

[Chorus]

I will survive! I will survive!
Cuz as long as I have batteries,
My sex life's gonna thrive!
I will always have good sex,
With a handful of latex!
I will survive! I will survive! Hey! Hey!

SUBJECT: ONE LINERS...

Definition of an Aussie husband: He hasn't kissed his wife for twenty years, but he will kill any man who does.

Fadden told Holt that his wife was driving him to drink. Holt thinks he's very lucky because his own wife makes him walk.

The late Bishop Scullin stated that the reason the Aussies fight so often among themselves is that they're always assured of having a worthy opponent.

An American lawyer asked, "Fadden, why is it that whenever you ask an Aussie a question, he answers with another question?"

"Who told you that?" asked Fadden.

Why are Aussie jokes so simple?
So the Poms can understand them.

Menzies went to trial for armed robbery. The jury foreman came out and announced, "Not guilty."

"That's grand!" shouted Menzies. "Does that mean I can keep the Money?"

Customer: "Could I be trying on that dress in the window?"
Shopkeeper: "I'd prefer that you use the dressing room."

What do you call an Australian male who knows how to control
a wife?
A bachelor.

Scullin: My wife has a terrible habit of staying up 'til two o'clock in
the morning. I can't break her of it.

Watson: What on earth is she doin' at that time?

Scullin: Waitin' for me to come home .

Fadden phoned the maternity ward at the hospital. "Quick!" He said.
"Send an ambulance, my wife is goin' to have a baby!"
"Tell me, is this her first baby?" the intern asked.
"No, this is her husband, Ned, speakin'."

"Watson," asked the chemist, "did that mudpack I gave you improve
your wife's appearance?"

"It did surely," replied Forde, "but it keeps fallin' off!"

SUBJECT: OBSERVATIONS AND CRAZY DEFINITIONS

From the *Washington Post* Style Invitational, in which it was postulated that English should have male and female nouns as many other languages have, and readers were asked to assign a gender to a noun of their choice and explain their reason.

Here are the best submissions:

SWISS ARMY KNIFE – MALE
Because even though it appears useful for a wide variety of work, it spends most of its time just opening bottles.

KIDNEYS – FEMALE
Because they always go to the bathroom in pairs.

TIRE – MALE
Because it goes bald and often is over inflated.

HOT AIR BALLOON – MALE
Because to get it to go anywhere you have to light a fire under it... and, of course, there's the hot air part.

SPONGES – FEMALE
Because they are soft and squeezable and retain water.

WEB PAGE – FEMALE
Because it is always getting hit on.

SHOE – MALE
Because it is usually unpolished, with its tongue hanging out.

COPIER – FEMALE
Because once turned off, it takes a while to warm up. Because it is an effective reproductive device when the right buttons are pushed. Because it can wreak havoc when the wrong buttons are pushed.

ZIPLOC BAGS – MALE
Because they hold everything in, but you can always see right through them.

continued...

SUBWAY – MALE
Because it uses the same old lines to pick people up.

HOURGLASS – FEMALE
Because over time, the weight shifts to the bottom.

HAMMER – MALE
Because it hasn't evolved much over the last 5,000 years, but it's handy to have around.

REMOTE CONTROL – FEMALE
...Ha! You thought I'd say male. But consider that it gives man pleasure, he'd be lost without it, and while he doesn't always know the right buttons to push, he keeps trying.

SUBJECT: ONLY IN HEAVEN

When Sister Mary died, she went to heaven.

St. Peter greeted her and explaind she had to answer a question to gain entry, despite her good living.

St. Peter asked, "What did Eve first say to Adam?"

Sister Mary thought and replied, "that's a hard one..."

St. Peter said, "Well done, welcome."

SUBJECT: OUCH...

A young man excitedly tells his mother he's fallen in love and is going to get married.

He says, "Just for fun, Ma, I'm going to bring over two other female friends in addition to my fiancée and you try and guess which one I'm going to marry."

The next day, he brings three beautiful women into the house and sits them down on the couch and they chat for a while.

He then says, "Okay, Ma, guess which one I'm going to marry."

She immediately replies, "The red head in the middle."

"That's amazing, Ma, You're right, how did you know?"

"I don't like her."

O

SUBJECT: ONE DAY IN THE CLASSROOM

A teacher gave her class of 11-year-olds an assignment:
Get their parents to tell them a story with a moral at the end of it.

The next day the kids came back and one by one began to tell their stories.

Ashley said, "My father's a farmer and we have a lot of egg laying hens. One time we were taking our eggs to market in a basket on the front seat of the car when we hit a big bump in the road and all the eggs went flying and broke and made a mess."

"What's the moral of the story?" asked the teacher.

"Don't put all your eggs in one basket!"

"Very good," said the teacher.

Next little Sarah raised her hand and said, "Our family are farmers too, but we raise chickens for the meat market. One day we had a dozen eggs, but when they hatched we only got ten live chicks, and the moral to this story is, 'Don't count your chickens before they're hatched'."

"That was a fine story Sarah. Michael, do you have a story to share?"

"Yes. My Daddy told me this story about my Aunt Karen."

"Aunt Karen was a flight engineer on a plane in the Gulf War and the plane got hit. She had to bail out over enemy territory and all she had was a bottle of whisky, a machine gun and a machete."

"She drank the whisky on the way down so it wouldn't break and then she landed right in the middle of 100 enemy troops. She killed seventy of them with the machine gun until she ran out of bullets. Then she killed twenty more with the machete until the blade broke. Then she killed the last ten with her bare hands."

"Good heavens," said the horrified teacher, "what kind of moral did your Daddy tell you from that horrible story?"

"Stay the hell away from Aunt Karen when she's been drinking."

SUBJECT: OXYMORONS

Happily Married

Passive Aggressive

Microsoft Works

Computer Jock

Government Organization

Pretty Ugly

Legally Drunk

Twelve Ounce Pound Cake

Child Proof

Diet Ice Cream

Working Vacation

Freezer Burn

Computer Security

Peace Force

New Classic

Extinct Life

○

SUBJECT: OLD DOGS... VERY WELL DONE

A wealthy old lady decides to go on a photo safari in Africa, taking her faithful aged poodle named Cuddles, along for the company.

One day the poodle starts chasing butterflies and before long, Cuddles discovers that she's lost. Wandering about, she notices a leopard heading rapidly in her direction with the intention of having lunch.

The old poodle thinks, "Oh, oh! I'm in deep doo doo now!" Noticing some bones on the ground close by, she immediately settles down to chew on the bones with her back to the approaching cat. Just as the leopard is about to leap, the old poodle exclaims loudly, "Boy, that was one delicious leopard! I wonder if there are any more around here?"

Hearing this, the young leopard halts his attack in mid-strike, a look of terror comes over him and he slinks away into the trees. "Whew!" says the leopard, "That was close! That old poodle nearly had me!"

Meanwhile, a monkey who had been watching the whole scene from a nearby tree, figures he can put this knowledge to good use and trade it for protection from the leopard. So off he goes, but the old poodle sees him heading after the leopard with great speed, and figures that something must be up. The monkey soon catches up with the leopard, spills the beans and strikes a deal for himself with the leopard.

The young leopard is furious at being made a fool of and says, "Here, monkey, hop on my back and see what's going to happen to that conniving canine!"

Now, the old poodle sees the leopard coming with the monkey on his back and thinks, "What am I going to do now?" but instead of running, the dog sits down with her back to her attackers, pretending she hasn't seen them yet, and just when they get close enough to hear, the old poodle says, "Where's that damn monkey? I sent him off an hour ago to bring me another leopard!"

Moral of this story... Don't mess with old farts... age and treachery will always overcome youth and skill! Bullshit and brilliance only come with age and experience!

SUBJECT: THE COUNTRY PASTOR

The poor country pastor was livid when he confronted his wife with the receipt for a $250 dress she had bought.

"How could you do this!" he exclaimed.

"I don't know," she wailed, "I was standing in the store looking at the dress. Then I found myself trying it on. It was like the Devil was whispering to me, "Gee, you look great in that dress. You should buy it.""

"Well," the pastor persisted, "You know how to deal with him! Just tell him, 'Get behind me, Satan!'"

"I did," replied his wife, "but then he said 'It looks great from back here, too.'"

SUBJECT: PRAYER

A Woman's Prayer:

Dear Lord,
I pray for wisdom, to understand a man, to love and to forgive him, and for patience, for his moods.

Because Lord, if I pray for strength, I'll just beat him to death.

SUBJECT: POETRY

Every day I give thanks to the Goddess,
I have two mounds upon my bodice,
I shave my legs, I sit down to pee,
I can justify any shopping spree.

Don't go to a barber, but a beauty salon,
Can get a massage, without a hard on.
I can balance my cheque book, can pump my own gas,
Can talk to my friends about the size of my own ass.

My beauty is a masterpiece, and yes it takes long,
At least I can admit to my friends where I went wrong.
I don't drive in circles at any cost,
And I don't have a problem admitting I'm lost.

Don't act like I'm in a timed marathon.
Every time I go to the john.
Don't brag about the size of my cup,
Hey, put the seat down, "cause I won't leave it up!"

I never forget an important date,
You just gotta deal with it, I'm usually late.
I don't watch movies with lots of gore,
And don't need an instant replay, to remember the score.

I won't lose my hair, or get jock itch,
And because I'm assertive, don't call me a 'bitch'
I don't wear the same underwear every day,
And the food in my fridge has no sign of decay.

Don't burp, don't belch, and certainly don't fart,
Ballet, not football I consider an art.
Flowers are okay, but jewellery is best,
Would you look at my face, and not my chest!

I don't have a problem expressing my feelings.
And I know when you're lying, you look at the ceiling.
Don't call me girl, babe or chick,
I am woman, get it, you p**k,

PS – So, just exactly what is a bitch????????
BABE IN TOTAL CONTROL OF HERSELF.

SUBJECT: THE PENSION

Having reached the age of 62, I went to apply for Canada Pension last week. After waiting in line for a very long time, I finally got to the counter. The woman there asked me for my driver's license to verify my age. I looked in my pockets and realized, to my great dismay, that I had left my wallet on the night stand in my bedroom. I told the lady that I was very sorry, but I seemed to have left my wallet at home. "I'll have to go get it and come back later," I said.

At that point, she said to me, "Unbutton your shirt."

I was confused, but I opened my shirt, revealing lots of curly silver hair. She said, "That silver hair on your chest is proof enough for me," and, with that, she promptly processed my application.

When I got home, I couldn't wait to tell my wife about my experience at the Canada Pension Office. She listened to the whole story and then said, "You should have dropped your pants. You might have gotten disability, too."

SUBJECT: THE PRIEST, PENTECOSTAL PREACHER AND THE RABBI

A priest, a Pentecostal preacher, and a Rabbi all served as chaplains to the students of the University of Montana in Missoula. They would get together two or three times a week for coffee and to talk shop.

One day, someone made the comment that preaching to people isn't really all that hard. A real challenge would be to preach to a bear. One thing led to another and they decided to do an experiment. They would all go out into the woods, find a bear, preach to it, and attempt to convert it.

Seven days later they're all together to discuss the experience.

Father Flannery, who has his arm in a sling, is on crutches, and has various bandages, goes first. "Well," he says, "I went into the woods to find me a bear. And when I found him I began to read to him from the Catechism. Well, that bear wanted nothing to do with me and began to slap me around. So I quickly grabbed my holy water, sprinkled him and, Holy God, he became as gentle as a lamb. The bishop is coming out next week to give him first communion and confirmation."

Reverend Billy Bob spoke next. He was in a wheelchair, with an arm and both legs in casts, and an IV drip. In his best fire and brimstone oratory he claimed, "WELL brothers, you KNOW that we don't sprinkle! I went out and I FOUND me a bear. And then I began to read to my bear from God's HOLY WORD! But that bear wanted nothing to do with me. So I took HOLD of him and we began to wrestle. We wrestled down one hill, UP another and DOWN another until we came to a creek. So I quick DUNKED him and BAPTIZED his hairy soul. And just like you said, he became as gentle as a lamb. We spent the rest of the day praising The Lord."

They both looked down at the rabbi, who was lying in a hospital bed. He was in a body cast and traction with IV's and monitors running in and out of him. He was in bad shape. The rabbi looks up and says, "Looking back on it, circumcision may not have been the best way to start."

SUBJECT: WHY PEOPLE ARE LIKE POTATOES...

Some people are very bossy and like to tell others what to do, but don't want to soil their own hands.
They are called 'DICK TATORS'

Some people never seem motivated to participate, but are just content to watch while others do the work.
They are called 'SPECK TATORS'

Some people never do anything to help, but are gifted at finding fault with the way others do the work.
They are called 'COMMENT TATORS'

Some people are always looking to cause problems by asking other to agree with them. It is too hot, or too cold, too sour or too sweet.
They are called 'AGIE TATORS'

There are those who say they will help, but somehow never get around to actually doing the promised help.
They are 'HEZZIE TATORS'

Some people can put up a front and pretend to be someone they are not.
They are called 'EMMA TATORS'

Then there are those who love and do what they say they will. They are always prepared to stop whatever they are doing and lend a helpful hand. They bring real sunshine into the lives of others.
They are called 'SWEET TATORS'.

SUBJECT: MORE PONDERINGS...

If your wife wants to learn to drive, don't stand in her way.

Algebra was easy for the Romans, X was always ten.

A truly happy person is the one who can enjoy the scenery on a detour.

Some mistakes are too much fun to only make once.

You may be only one person in the world, but you may also be the world to one person.

October is a bad month to speculate on the stock market. Other poor months are January, March, May, September, November, February, April, June, August and December.

Don't cry because it is over, smile because it happened.

It's better to have loved and lost than to do 20 kilo's of washing a week.

Dieting is a matter of mind over platter.

If vegetarians eat vegetables, what do humanitarians eat?

Why is it, when a door is open it's ajar, but when a jar is open it's not a door.

Why do we wash bath towels,? Aren't we clean when we use them?.

Why doesn't Tarzan have a beard?.

How come Superman could stop bullets but ducked when someone threw a gun at him?

What do little birdies see, when they get knocked unconscious?

When a man talks dirty to a woman, it's sexual harassment. When a woman taks dirty to man, it's $4.95 per minute.

If it's tourist season, why can't we shoot them?

Why is a carrot more orange than an orange?

Why are there five syllables in the word 'monosyllabic'?

SUBJECT: PROFESSOR AND THE STUDENT

A Professor was giving a big test one day to his students.

He handed out all the tests and went to his desk to wait.
Once the test was over, the students all handed the tests back in.
The professor noticed that one of the students had attached $100 note to his test, with a note saying 'A dollar per point'.

The next class the professor handed the tests back out.

This student got his test and $56 change.

SUBJECT: A GOOD PUN IS ITS OWN REWORD

- Energizer Bunny arrested – charged with battery.

- A pessimist's blood type is always B negative.

- Practice safe eating – always use condiments.

- I used to work in a blanket factory, but it folded.

- If electricity comes from electrons... does that mean that morality comes from morons?

- Marriage is the mourning after the knot before.

- Corduroy pillows are making headlines.

- Sea captains don't like crew cuts.

- A gossip is someone with a great sense of rumour.

- Without geometry, life is pointless.

- When you dream in colour, it's a pigment of your imagination.

Atilla the pun

SUBJECT: PROFESSORS' DEFINITIONS OF A KISS

Professors of different subjects define the same word in different ways:

Prof. of Computer Science
A kiss is a few bits of love compiled into a byte.

Prof. of Algebra
A kiss is two divided by nothing.

Prof. of Geometry
A kiss is the shortest distance between two straight lines.

Prof. of Physics
A kiss is the contraction of mouth due to the expansion of the heart.

Prof. of Chemistry
A kiss is the reaction of the interaction between two hearts.

Prof. of Zoology
A kiss is the interchange of unisexual salivary bacteria.

Prof. of Physiology
A kiss is the juxtaposition of two orbicular ors muscles in the state of contraction.

Prof. of Dentistry
A kiss is infectious and antiseptic.

Prof. of Accountancy
A kiss is a credit because it is profitable when returned.

Prof. of Economics
A kiss is that thing for which the demand is higher than the supply.

Prof. of Statistics
A kiss is an event whose probability depends on the vital statistics of 36-24-36.

Prof. of Philosophy
A kiss is the persecution for the child, ecstasy for the youth and homage for the old.

Prof. of English:
A kiss is a noun that is used as a conjunction. It is more common than proper. It is spoken in the plural and it is applicable to all.

SUBJECT: THE PHARMACY

Mrs Jones walked into her small town pharmacy and said she wanted to by some cyanide.

The pharmacist said, "Why in the world do you need do buy cyanide?"

Mrs Jones then explained she needed to poison her husband. The pharmacist's eyes got big, and he said, "Lord have Mercy. I can't give you cyanide to kill you husband! That's against the law. I'll lose my license, they'll throw us both in jail, and...and all kinds of bad things will happen! Absolutely not: you can not have any cyanide!"

Mrs Jones reached into her purse and pulled out a picture of her husband in bed with the pharmacist's wife.

The pharmacist looked at the picture and replied, "Well, now, you didn't tell me you had a prescription."

SUBJECT: POINTS TO PONDER

1. Marriage changes passion. Suddenly you're in bed with a relative.

2. I saw a woman wearing a sweat shirt with 'Guess' on it. So I said, "Implants?" She hit me.

3. I don't do drugs. I get the same effect just standing up fast.

4. I live in my own little world. But it's OK. They know me here.

5. I got a sweater for Christmas. I really wanted a screamer or moaner.

6. If flying is so safe, why do they call the airport the terminal?

7. I don't approve of political jokes. I've seen too many of them get elected.

8. I love being married. It's so great to find that one special person you want to annoy for the rest of your life.

9. I am a nobody, and nobody is perfect; therefore, I am perfect.

10. Everyday I beat my own previous record for number of consecutive days I have stayed alive.

11. How come we choose from just two people to run for president and 50 for Miss America?

12. Isn't having a smoking section in a restaurant like having a peeing section in a swimming pool?

13. Why is it that most nudists are people you don't want to see naked?

14. Snowmen fall from Heaven unassembled.

15. Every time I walk into a singles bar I can hear Mum's wise words, "Don't pick that up, you don't know where it's been!"

16. A good friend will come and bail you out of jail... but, a true friend will be sitting next to you saying, "Damn... that was fun!"

17. I signed up for an exercise class and was told to wear loose–fitting clothing. If I HAD any loose–fitting clothing, I wouldn't have signed up in the first place!

18. When I was young we used to go 'skinny dipping', now I just 'chunky dunk'.

19. The worst thing about accidents in the kitchen is eating them.

20. Don't argue with an idiot; people watching may not be able to tell the difference.

21. Wouldn't it be nice if whenever we messed up our life we could simply press 'Ctrl Alt Delete' and start all over?

22. Stress is when you wake up screaming and then you realize you haven't fallen asleep yet.

23. My husband says I never listen to him (at least I think that's what he said).

SUBJECT: ADVENTURE'S IN PUNCTUATION HAVE YOU EVER WONDERED WHY GRAMMAR IS IMPORTANT

Dear John:

I want a man who knows what love is all about.

You are generous, kind, thoughtful. People who are not like you admit to being useless and inferior. You have ruined me for other men. I yearn for you. I have no feelings whatsoever when we're apart. I can be forever happy-will you let me be yours?

Jane

Dear John:

I want a man who knows what love is. All about you are generous, kind, thoughtful people, who are not like you. Admit to being useless and inferior. You have ruined me. For other men, I yearn. For you, I have no feelings whatsoever. When we're apart, I can be forever happy. Will you let me be?

Yours,
Jane

SUBJECT: PILOTS...

Two men dressed in pilots' uniforms walk up the aisle of
the aeroplane.

Both are wearing dark glasses, one is using a guide dog, and the
other is tapping his way along the aisle with a cane. Nervous
laughter spreads through the cabin, but the men enter the cockpit,
the door closes, and the engines start up. The passengers begin
glancing nervously around, searching for some sign that this is just a
little practical joke. None is forthcoming.

The plane moves faster and faster down the runway, and the people
sitting in the window seats realize they're headed straight for the
water – at the edge of the airport runway. As it begins to look as
though the plane will plough into the water, panicked screams fill
the cabin. At that moment, the plane lifts smoothly into the air. The
passengers relax and laugh a little sheepishly, and soon all retreat
into their magazines, secure in the knowledge that the plane is
obviously in good hands.

In the cockpit, one of the blind pilots turns to the other and says,
"You know, Bob, one of these days, they're gonna scream too late and
we're all gonna die."

SUBJECT: WOMAN'S PRAYER

Lord,
Before I lay me down to sleep,
I pray for a man, who's not a creep.
One who is handsome, smart and strong,
One who's willy is, thick and long,
One who thinks before he speaks,
When he promises to call, he won't wait for weeks.
I pray that he is gainfully employed,
And when I spend his cash, he won't be annoyed.
Pulls out my chair, and opens the door,
Massages my back and then begs for more.
Oh! Send me a man, who'll make love to my mind,
Knows just what to say, when I ask, "How big is my behind?"
One who'll make love till my body is a twitchin',
In the hall, the loo, the garden, the kitchen!
I pray that this man will love me no end,
And never attempt to shag my best friend.
And as I kneel and pray by my bed,
I look at the creep you sent me instead.
Amen.

SUBJECT: GETTING THE PRIORITIES RIGHT

Jacob, age 92, and Rebecca, age 89, living in Florida, are all excited about their decision to get married. They go for a stroll to discuss the wedding. On the way they pass a drugstore. Jacob suggests they go in.

Jacob addresses the man behind the counter.

Jacob:	"Are you the owner?"
Pharmacist:	"Yes, Sir."

Jacob:	"We're about to get married. Do you sell heart medication?"
Pharmacist:	"Of course we do."

Jacob:	"How about medicine for circulation?"
Pharmacist:	"All kinds."

Jacob:	"Medicine for rheumatism and scoliosis?"
Pharmacist:	"Definitely."

Jacob:	"How about Viagra?"
Pharmacist:	"Of course."

Jacob:	"Medicine for memory problems, arthritis, jaundice?"
Pharmacist:	"Yes, a large variety."

Jacob:	"What about vitamins, sleeping pills, Geritol, antidotes for Parkinson's disease?"
Pharmacist:	"Absolutely."

Jacob:	"You sell wheelchairs and walkers?"
Pharmacist:	"All speeds and sizes."

Jacob:	"We'd like to use this store as our Bridal Registry."

SUBJECT: PICK A STARTING SALARY...

Reaching the end of the job interview, the Human Resources Manger asked the young MBA fresh out of MIT, "And what starting salary are you looking for?"

The candidate said, "In the neighbourhood of $125,000 a year, depending on the benefits package."

The HR Manager said, "Well, what would you say to a package of five weeks vacation, 14 days paid holiday, full medical and dental, company matching retirement fund of 50 per cent of salary, and a company car leased every two years – say, a silver BMW."

The engineer sat straight up and said, "Wow!!! Are you kidding?" The HR manager said, "Certainly, ... but you started it."

The HR manager, had to be female.

SUBJECT: THE PARROT

This nice old Jewish lady went decided to buy a parrot so she went to the store and bought one. The parrot seemed fine and when Friday night came, she dressed the parrot up and went to the temple.

The parrot seemed fine but when the Rabbi went to bless the congregation, the parrot screamed out, "It's friggin cold in here!"

The woman, completely appalled, grabbed the parrot and ran out. Well, the parrot seemed fine for the next week so once again, on Friday she and the parrot got dressed up and went to the temple.

Like the previous week, the parrot was fine until the Rabbi went to bless the congregation at which the parrot, once again, screamed out, "It's friggin cold in here!"

Once again, the lady was appalled, grabbed the parrot and ran out of temple. She decided to confront the man at the pet store to see what was going on. The clerk at the pet store said, "You gotta show the parrot who's boss so next time he does this, grab him by his legs and swing him around your head a few times. That should teach him a lesson."

That Friday night they once again got dressed up and went to the temple. Like the previous two weeks, when the Rabbi went to bless the congregation, the parrot screamed out, "It's friggin cold in here!"

The lady, remembering what the clerk said, grabbed the parrot by its legs and swung it around her head a few times. When she was done, the parrot looked at her and screamed out, "And friggin windy, too."

SUBJECT: PADDY

Paddy's pregnant sister was in a terrible car accident and went into a deep coma.

After being in the coma for nearly six months, she wakes up and sees that she is no longer pregnant. Frantically, she asks the doctor about her baby. The doctor replies, "Ma'am, you had twins! A boy and a girl."

"The babies are fine now however they were poorly at birth and had to be christened immediately – your brother came in and named them."

The woman thinks to herself, "Oh suffering Jesus no, not me brother... he's a fecking, clueless, gobsh*te!" Expecting the worst, she asks the doctor, "Well, what's my daughter's name?"

"Denise," says the doctor.

The new mother is somewhat relieved, "Wow, That's a beautiful name, I guess I was wrong about my brother... I like Denise."

Then she asks, "What's the boy's name?
"Denephew"

SUBJECT: HOW ABOUT TAKING
A QUICK QUIZ? PAY ATTENTION!

1. What is five divided by 1/2 plus three?

2. I have two coins making 55 cents but one is not a nickel. How can that be?

3. Why are 1977 dollars worth more than 1976 dollars?

4. What word in the English language does nearly everyone pronounce incorrectly?

5. In the United States is it legal for a man to marry his widow's sister?

6. How much dirt is there in a hole that measures two feet by three feet by four feet?

7. Some months have 30 days, some months have 31 days. How many have 28?

8. Which is correct – eight and eight IS fifteen or eight and eight ARE fifteen?

9. A ten foot rope ladder hangs over the side of a boat with the bottom rung at the surface of the water. There is one foot between rungs and the tide goes up at the rate of 6 inches per hour. How long until three rungs are covered?

10. Mr. and Mrs Smith have six daughters and each daughter has one brother. How many people in the family?

Answers on page 182

SUBJECT: QUICKIES...

What do men and rolls of carpet have in common?
Lay them properly the first time and you can walk all over them, for the rest of their lives.

What is the smartest thing a man can say?
"My wife says..."

What's the difference between pink and purple?
How good the grip.

It's okay to let him think, he wears the trousers.
As long as you tell him what pair to put on.

Answers from page 181
1. 13. 5 divided by .5 = 10 + 3 = 13;
2. Only one is not a nickel, because it is a 50 cent piece. The other is a nickel;
3. Because $1977 is more than $1976;
4. The word 'incorrectly';
5. No. If he has a widow, then the man is dead and cannot marry anyone;
6. There is no dirt in a hole;
7. All the months;
8. Neither. Eight and eight equals SIXTEEN;
9. The rungs will never be covered because the boat rises with the tide;
10. 9 family members total. 6 daughters, 1 brother and Mr. Smith and Mrs Smith.

SUBJECT: AUSTRALIAN RADIO
THIS IS ABSOLUTELY HILARIOUS !!!

Just imagine sitting in traffic on your way to work and hearing this.

Many Sydney folks did hear this on the FOX FM morning show. The DJs play a game where they award winners great prizes.

The game is called *Mate Match*. The DJs call someone at work and ask if they are married or seriously involved with someone. If the contestant answers, "Yes," he or she is then asked three random yet highly personal questions.

The person is also asked to divulge the name of their partner (with phone number) for verification. If their partner answers those same three questions correctly, they both win the prize. One particular game, however, several months ago made the City of Big Shoulders drop to its knees with laughter and is possibly the funniest thing I've heard yet.

Anyway, here's how it all went down:

DJ: "Hey! This is Ed on FOX-FM. Have you ever heard of *Mate Match*?"

Contestant: (laughing) "Yes, I have."

DJ: "Great! Then you know we're giving away a trip to the Gold Coast if you win. What is your name? First only please."

Contestant: "Brian."

DJ: "Brian, are you married or what?"

Brian: "Yes."

DJ: "Yes? Does that mean you're married or you're what?"

Brian: (laughing nervously) "Yes, I am married."

DJ: "Thank you. Now, what is your wife's name? First only please."

Brian: "Sara."

continued...

DJ:	"Is Sara at work, Brian?"
Brian:	"She is gonna kill me."
DJ:	"Stay with me here, Brian! Is she at work?"
Brian:	(laughing) "Yes, she's at work."
DJ:	"Okay, first question – when was the last time you had sex?"
Brian:	"She is gonna kill me."
DJ:	"Brian! Stay with me here!"
Brian:	"About eight o'clock this morning."
DJ:	"Atta boy, Brian."
Brian:	(laughing sheepishly) "Well..."
DJ:	"Question two – How long did it last?"
Brian:	"About ten minutes."
DJ:	"Wow! You really want that trip, huh? No one would ever have said that if a trip wasn't at stake."
Brian:	"Yeah, that trip sure would be nice."
DJ:	"Okay. Final question. Where did you have sex at eight o'clock this morning?"
Brian:	(laughing hard) "I, ummm, I, well..."
DJ:	"This sounds good, Brian. Where was it at?"
Brian:	"Not that it was all that great, but her Mum is staying with us for a couple of weeks..."
DJ:	"Uh huh..."
Brian:	"...and the Mother–In–Law was in the shower at the time."
DJ:	"Atta boy, Brian."
Brian:	"On the kitchen table."
DJ:	"Not that great?? That is more adventure than the previous hundred times I've done it. Okay folks, I will put Brian on hold, get this wife's work number and call her up. You listen to this."

THE OFFICE INBOX JOKE BOOK – JOKES FOR HER

Three minutes of commercials follow.

DJ:	"Okay audience, let's call Sarah, shall we?" (touch tones... ringing...)
Clerk:	"Kinkos."
DJ:	"Hey, is Sarah around there somewhere?"
Clerk:	"This is she."
DJ:	"Sarah, this is Ed with FOX–FM. We are live on the air right now and I've been talking with Brian for a couple of hours now."
Sarah:	(laughing) "A couple of hours?"
DJ:	"Well, a while now. He is on the line with us. Brian knows not to give any answers away or you'll lose. Sooooooo... do you know the rules of *Mate Match*?"
Sarah:	"No."
DJ:	"Good!"
Brian:	(laughing)
Sarah:	(laughing) "Brian, what the hell are you up to?"
Brian:	(laughing) "Just answer his questions honestly, okay? Be completely honest."
DJ:	"Yeah yeah yeah. Sure. Now, I will ask you three questions, Sarah. If your answers match Brian's answers, then the both of you will be off to the Gold Coast for five days on us.
Sarah:	(laughing) "Yes."
DJ:	"Alright. When did you last have sex, Sarah?"
Sarah:	"Oh God, Brian... uh, this morning before Brian went to work."
DJ:	"What time?"
Sarah:	"Around eight this morning."
DJ:	"Very good. Next question. How long did it last?"
Sarah:	"12, 15 minutes maybe."

continued...

| **DJ:** | "Hmmmm. That's close enough. I am sure she is trying to protect his manhood. We've got one last question, Sarah. You are one question away from a trip to the Gold Coast. Are you ready?" |
| **Sarah:** | (laughing) "Yes." |

DJ:	"Where did you have it?"
Sarah:	"OH MY GOD, BRIAN!! You didn't tell them that, did you?"
Brian:	"Just tell him, honey."

| **DJ:** | "What is bothering you so much, Sarah?" |
| **Sarah:** | "Well..." |

| **DJ:** | "Come on Sarah... where did you have it?" |
| **Sarah:** | "Up the arse..." |

After a long pause, the DJ said: "Folks, we need to take station break"

SUBJECT: REQUEST FOR A PAY RISE

I, the Penis,
hereby request a raise in salary for the following reasons:

I do physical labour.
I work in great depths.
I plunge head first into everything I do.
I do not get weekends or holidays off.
I work in a damp environment.
I work in a dark work place that has poor ventilation.
I work in high temperatures.
My work exposes me to contagious diseases.

Sincerely,
The Penis

Dear Penis,
After considering the arguments you have raised, the administration rejects your request for the following reasons:

You do not work eight hours straight.
You fall asleep after brief work periods.
You do not always follow the orders of the management team.
You do not stay in your designated area and are often seen visiting other locations.
You do not take initiative.
You need to be pressured and stimulated in order to start working.
You leave the work place rather messy at the end of your shift.
You don't always observe necessary safety regulations, such as wearing the correct protective clothing.
You will retire well before you are 65.
You are unable to work double shifts.
You sometimes leave your designated work area before you have completed your assigned task.
You spit at your customers.

And if that were not enough, you are constantly seen entering and exiting the work place carrying two suspicious looking bags.

Sincerely,
The Management

SUBJECT: LIGHT RELIEF...

What has 300 legs and 26 teeth?
The front row of a Willie Nelson concert.

Did you hear about the guy who fell into a glass grinder?
He made a spectacle of himself.

I went to a Seafood Disco,
and ended up pulling a mussel.

What do vegetarian cannibals eat?
Swedes!

Tragedy – Cessna crashes into Irish Cemetery
387 bodies recovered so far.

Did you hear about the lepers poker game?
One threw in his hand, the others laughed their heads off.

What did the zero say to the eight?
Nice belt.

What's a wok?
Something you kill a wabbit wiff when you don't have a wifle.

SUBJECT: THE RABBIT

A man is driving along a highway and sees a rabbit jump out across the middle of the road. He swerves to avoid hitting it, but unfortunately the rabbit jumps right in front of the car.

The driver, a sensitive man as well as an animal lover, pulls over and gets out to see what has become of the rabbit. Much to his dismay, the rabbit is dead. The driver feels so awful that he begins to cry.

A beautiful blonde woman driving down the highway sees a man crying on the side of the road and pulls over. She steps out of the car and asks the man what's wrong. "I feel terrible," he explains, "I accidentally hit this rabbit and killed it."

The blonde says, "Don't worry." She runs to her car and pulls out a spray can. She walks over to the limp, dead rabbit, bends down, and sprays the contents onto the rabbit.

The rabbit jumps up, waves its paw at the two of them and hops off down the road. Ten feet away the rabbit stops, turns around and waves again, he hops down the road another ten feet, turns and waves, hops another ten feet, turns and waves, and repeats this again and again and again, until he hops out of sight.

The man is astonished. He runs over to the woman and demands, "What is in that can? What did you spray on that rabbit?"

The woman turns the can around so that the man can read the label. It says...

(Are you ready for this?)
(Are you sure?)
(This is bad!)
(It's definitely a Blonde Joke!)
(You know you could just click off and not read the punch line...)
(You know you're gonna be sorry)
(Last chance)
(OK, here it is)
It says,

"Hair Spray – Restores life to dead hair, adds permanent wave."

SUBJECT: THEY ASK WHY I LIKE RETIREMENT

Q: How many days in a week?
A: 6 Saturdays, one Sunday

Q: When is a retiree's bedtime?
A: Three hours after he falls asleep on the couch.

Q: How many retirees to change a light bulb?
A: Only one, but it might take all day.

Q: What's the biggest gripe of retirees?
A: There is not enough time to get everything done.

Q: Why don't retirees mind being called Seniors?
A: The term comes with a ten per cent discount.

Q: Among retirees what is considered formal attire?
A: Tied shoes.

Q: Why do retirees count pennies?
A: They are the only ones who have the time.

Q: What is the common term for someone who enjoys work and refuses to retire?
A: NUTS!

Q: Why are retirees so slow to clean out the basement, attic or garage?
A: They know that as soon as they do, one of their adult kids will want to store stuff there.

Q: What do retirees call a long lunch?
A: Normal.

Q: What is the best way to describe retirement?
A: The never ending Coffee Break.

Q: What's the biggest advantage of going back to school as a retiree?
A: If you cut classes, no one calls your parents.

SUBJECT: SMILE AND SMILE

At times the word arrangements in church bulletins produce hilarious reading.

Here are some examples. All are authentic announcements in churches.

- This afternoon there will be a meeting in the North and South ends of this church. Children will be baptised both ends.

- Tuesday at 4 p.m. there will be an Ice Cream Social. All ladies giving milk please come early.

- Wednesday, the Ladies Literary Society will meet. Mrs Johnson will sing *Put Me in a Little Bed* accompanied by the Pastor.

- Thursday at 5 p.m. there will be a meeting of the Little Mothers' Club. All wishing to become Little Mothers will please meet the Priest in his study.

- This being Easter Sunday, we will ask Mrs Brown to come forward and lay an egg on the Alter.

- The services today will end with *Little Drops of Water*. One of the men will start quietly and the rest of the congregation will join in.

- The ladies of the church have cast off the clothing of every kind, and they can be seen in the church basement on Friday afternoon.

- On Sunday, a special collection will be taken to defray the expense of the new carpet. All wishing to do something on the carpet please come forward and get a piece of paper.

- Tonight's Sermon 'What is Hell?'. Come early and listen to our choir practice.

SUBJECT: NEVER TAKE A MAN SHOPPING IN TARGET

The following letter was sent to a long time patron of a local Target store. After receiving this letter, she vowed that she would NEVER take her husband shopping with her again! ! !

January 12, 2006

Re: Mr. Bill Fenton Multiple Complaints

Dear Mrs Fenton,

Over the past six months, your husband, Mr. Bill Fenton, has been causing quite a commotion in our store. We cannot tolerate this type of behaviour and have considered banning the entire family from shopping in any of our stores. We have documented all incidents on our video surveillance equipment.

Three of our clerks are attending counselling from the trouble your husband has caused. All complaints against Mr. Fenton have been compiled and are listed below.

15 Things Mr. Bill Fenton has done while his spouse is shopping:

1. June 15: Took four boxes of condoms and randomly put them in people's carts when they weren't looking.

2. July 2: Set all the alarm clocks in homewares to go off at five-minute intervals.

3. July 7: Made a trail of tomato juice on the floor leading to the bathrooms.

4. July 19: Walked up to an employee and told her in an official tone, 'Code Three' in homewares... and watched what happened.

5. August 4: Went to the Service Desk and asked to put a bag of M&Ms on lay-away.

6. September 14: Moved a 'CAUTION – WET FLOOR' sign to a carpeted area.

7. September 15: Set up a tent in the camping department and told other shoppers he'd invite them in if they'll bring pillows from the bedding department.

8. September 23: When a clerk asks if they can help him, he begins to cry and asks, "Why can't you people just leave me alone?"

9. October 4: Looked right into the security camera, used it as a mirror, and picked his nose.

10. November 10: While handling guns in the hunting department, asked the clerk if he knows where the antidepressants are.

11. December 3: Darted around the store suspiciously loudly humming the *Mission Impossible* theme.

12. December 6: In the auto department, practised his, 'Madonna look' using different size funnels.

13. December 18: Hid in a clothing rack and when people browse through, yelled, "PICK ME! PICK ME!"

14. December 21: When an announcement came over the loud speaker, he assumes the foetal position and screams, "NO! NO! It's those voices again!!!!"

(And last, but not least!)

15. December 23: Went into a fitting room, shut the door and waited awhile, then, yelled, very loudly, "There is no toilet paper in here!"

SUBJECT: STRICTLY WOMEN'S BUSINESS

A true story as told on Melbourne Radio.

I was due later that week for an appointment with the Gynaecologist. When early that morning I received a call from his office, I had been re-scheduled for early that morning at 9.30 a.m. I had only just packed everyone off to work and school it was 8.45 a.m. already. The car trip usually took about 30 minutes, so I didn't have time to spare.

As most women do, I'm sure, I like to take a little extra effort over hygiene when making such visits, but this time I wasn't going to be able to make the full effort. Rushing upstairs, threw off my dressing gown, wet the flannel and gave myself a wash in the basin. Taking extra care to make sure I was presentable... threw the flannel in the wash basket, dressed, hopped in the car and raced to my appointment.

I was called in promptly and knowing the procedure, as I'm sure you all do, hopped up on the table, looked over the other side of the room and pretended I was in Hawaii or some place thousands of miles away.

I was a little surprised when he said, "My we have taken a little extra effort this morning haven't we?" Appointment over, I heaved a sigh and went home. The rest of the day was normal.

At 7.30 p.m. that evening, my eldest daughter was fixing herself to go to a school dance, when she called out down stairs from the bathroom, "Mum where is my flannel" I called back to her to "get another from the linen cupboard."

She called back, "No I need, my one that was here by the basin... it had all my glitter and sparkles in it."

SUBJECT: SAN DIEGO CHIMPS

A blonde lady motorist was about two hours from San Diego when she was flagged down by a man whose truck had broken down.

The man walked up to the car and asked, "Are you going to San Diego?"

"Sure," answered the blonde, "do you need a lift? "

"Not for me. I'll be spending the next three hours fixing my truck. My problem is I've got two chimpanzees in the back which have to be taken to the San Diego Zoo. They're a bit stressed already so I don't want to keep them on the road all day. Could you possibly take them to the zoo for me? I'll give you $100 for your trouble."

"I'd be happy to," said the blonde.

So the two chimpanzees were ushered into the back seat of the blonde's car and carefully strapped into their seat belts. Off they went.

Five hours later, the truck driver was driving through the heart of San Diego when suddenly he was horrified!!

There was the blonde walking down the street and holding hands with the two chimps, much to the amusement of a big crowd. With a screech of brakes he pulled off the road and ran over to the blonde.

"What the heck are you doing here?" he demanded, "I gave you $100 to take these chimpanzees to the zoo."

"Yes, I know you did," said the blonde, "but we had money left over – so now we're going to Sea World."

SUBJECT: SCENARIO

You are driving in a car at a constant speed.

On your left side is a valley and on your right side is a fire engine travelling at the same speed as you.

In front of you is a galloping pig which is the same size as your car and you cannot overtake it.

Behind you is a helicopter flying at ground level.

Both the giant pig and the helicopter are also travelling at the same speed as you.

What must you do to safely get out of this highly dangerous situation?

SUBJECT: SALVATION ARMY...

A guy arrives at a Durban Hotel checks in and tells the desk clerk to send up a bottle of good champagne and a woman to his room.

In a short while, someone knocks on his door. When he opens it, there stands a lady in a Salvation Army uniform. He looks surprised but invites her in.

She says, "You asked for a lady, didn't you?" He says, "Well, Yes." So she begins to disrobe. When she is almost undressed, she stops suddenly and says, "By the way, are you married or single?"

He says, "I'm married."

She immediately starts to put all her clothes back on. "What now?" he asks.

Her reply, "We cater strictly for the needy, not the greedy."

SUBJECT: THINGS STRESSED OUT WOMEN SAY AT WORK...

1. Okay, okay! I take it back. Un-stuff you.

2. You say I'm a bitch like it's a bad thing.

3. Well this day was a total waste of make up.

4. Well, aren't we a damn ray of sunshine?

5. Don't bother me, I'm living happily ever after.

6. Do I look like a people person?

7. This isn't an office. It's hell with fluorescent lighting.

8. I started out with nothing and I still have most of it left.

9. Therapy is expensive. Popping bubble wrap is cheap. You choose.

10. Why don't you try practising random acts of intelligence and senseless acts of self-control?

11. I'm not crazy. I've been in a very bad mood for 30 years.

12. Sarcasm is just one more service I offer.

13. Do they ever shut up on your planet?

14. I'm not your type. I'm not inflatable.

15. Back off!! You're standing in my aura.

16. Don't worry, I forgot your name too.

17. I work 45 hours a week to be this poor.

18. Not all men are annoying. Some are dead.

19. Wait... I'm trying to imagine you with a personality.

20. Chaos, panic and disorder... my work here is done.

21. Ambivalent? Well, yes and no.

22. You look like hell. Is that the style now?

23. Earth is full. Go home.

24. Aw, did I step on your poor itty bitty ego?

25. I'm not tense, just terribly, terribly alert.

26. A hard–on doesn't count as personal growth.

27. You are depriving some village of an idiot.

28. If idiots could fly, this place would be an airport.

29. Look in my eyes... do you see one ounce of who-gives-a-shit?

SUBJECT: SHOPPING AT MYERS...

A woman goes into Myers to buy a rod and reel for her grandson's birthday.

She doesn't know which one to get, so she just grabs one and goes over to the counter. The Myers salesman is standing there, wearing dark shades. She says, "Excuse me. Can you tell me anything about this rod and reel?"

He says, "Madam, I'm completely blind, but, if you'll drop it on the counter, I can tell you everything you need to know about it from the sound it makes."

She doesn't believe him but drops it on the counter anyway.

He says, "That's a six-foot Shakespeare graphite rod with a Zebco 404 reel and ten pound test line. It's a good all around combination, and it's on sale this week for $44."

She says, "It's amazing that you can tell all that just by the sound of it dropping on the counter. I'll take it!" As she opens her purse, her credit card drops on the floor. "Oh, that sounds like a Visa card," he says.

As the lady bends down to pick up the card, she accidentally farts. At first she is really embarrassed but then realizes there is no way the blind salesman could tell it was she who had farted.

The man rings up the sale and says, "That'll be $58.50 please." The woman is totally confused by this and asks, "Didn't you tell me It was on sale for $44. How did you get to $58.50?"

"The Duck Caller is $11 and the Fish Bait is $3.50."

SUBJECT: STRANGE AND FUNNY SIGNS

At a Gynaecologist's Office
"Dr. Jones, at your cervix.

At a Proctologist's door
"To expedite your visit please back in."

At an Optometrist's office:
"If you don't see what you're looking for, you've come
to the right place."

In a Podiatrist's office:
"Time wounds all heels."

In a Restaurant window:
"Don't stand there and be hungry, come on in and get fed up.

SUBJECT: SHOPPING

A woman was in a sex boutique shopping for vibrators when the
clerk said, "Perhaps you might be interested in this one. It's our
most realistic model." The woman said, "You mean it's shaped
exactly like a man's penis?" "No," the clerk replied, "I mean that
after five minutes it goes soft for the rest of the night."

SUBJECT: SAD BUT TRUE

And we thought the Oz education system needed an overhaul...

Game show answers from the United Kingdom, *The Weakest Link*, BBC1/BBC2

Anne Robinson: "In traffic, what 'J' is where two roads meet?"
Contestant: "Jool carriageway."

Robinson: "Which Italian city is overlooked by Vesuvius?"
Contestant: "Bombay."

Robinson: "What insect is commonly found hovering above lakes?"
Contestant: "Crocodiles."
Robinson: "Wh...?"
Contestant: (interrupting) "Pass!"

Robinson: "In olden times, what were minstrels, travelling entertainers or chocolate salesmen?"
Contestant: "Chocolate salesmen."

Robinson: "The Bible: in the New Testament, the Four Gospels were written by Matthew, Mark, Luke and...?"
Contestant: (long pause) "Joe?"

National Lottery Jet Set, BBC1

Eamonn Holmes: "What's the name of the playwright commonly known by the initials G.B.S.?"
Contestant: "William Shakespeare."

Chris Searle Show, BBC Radio Bristol

Searle: "In which European country is Mount Etna?"
Caller: "Japan."

continued...

| Searle: | "I did say which European country, so in case you didn't hear that, I can let you try again." |
| Caller: | "Er... Mexico?" |

Family Fortunes, ITV

1. **Something a blind man might use?**
   A Sword
2. **A Song with the word Moon in the title?**
   Blue Suede Moon
3. **Name the Capital of France?**
   F
4. **Name a bird with a long neck?**
   Naomi Campbell
5. **Name an occupation where you might need a torch?**
   A burglar
6. **Where is the Taj Mahal?**
   Opposite the Dental Hospital
7. **What is Hitler's first name?**
   Heil
8. **A famous Scotsman?**
   Jock
9. **Some famous brothers?**
   Bonnie and Clyde.
10. **A dangerous race?**
    The Arabs
11. **Something that floats in a bath?**
    Water
12. **An item of clothing worn by the Three Musketeers?**
    A horse
13. **Something you wear on a beach?**
    A deck chair
14. **A famous Royal?**
    Mail
15. **Something that flies that doesn't have an engine?**
    A bicycle with wings
16. **A famous bridge?**
    The Bridge Over Troubled Waters
17. **Something a cat does?**
    Goes to the toilet
18. **Something you do in the bathroom?**
    Decorate

19. **A method of securing your home?**
    Put the kettle on
20. **Something associated with pigs?**
    The police
21. **A sign of the Zodiac?**
    April
22. **Something people might be allergic to?**
    Skiing
23. **Something you do before you go to bed?**
    Sleep
24. **Something you put on walls?**
    A roof
25. **Something Slippery?**
    A con man
26. **A kind of ache?**
    A fillet of fish
27. **A Jacket Potato topping?**
    Jam
28. **A food that can be brown or white?**
    A potato
29. **Something sold by gypsies?**
    Bananas
30. **Something Red?**
    My sweater

The Afternoon Programme Quiz, ABC 774

Presenter:	Who killed Cock Robin?
Contestant:	Oh God, I didn't even know he was dead.

Lincs FM phone-in

Presenter:	Which is the largest Spanish–speaking country in the world?
Contestant:	Barcelona.
Presenter:	I was really after the name of a country.
Contestant:	I'm sorry, I don't know the names of any countries in Spain.

----

continued...

Steve Wright Show, Radio 2

Wright: On which continent would you find the River Danube?
Contestant: India.

Wright: What is the Italian word for motorway?
Contestant: Espresso.

Wright: What is the capital of Australia? And it's not Sydney.
Contestant: Sydney.

Wright: What was the animal referred to in Val Doonican's song Paddy McGinty's?
Contestant: I don't know.
Wright: It begins with a 'G'.
Contestant: Cow.

This Morning, ITV

Judy Finnegan: The American TV show *The Sopranos* is about opera. True or false?
Contestant: True?
Finnegan: No, actually, it's about the Mafia. But it is an American TV show, so I'll give you that.

BBC Radio Newcastle

Paul Wappat: How long did the Six Day War between Egypt and Israel last?
Contestant: (after long pause) Fourteen days.

Bob Hope Birthday Quiz, LBC

Presenter: Bob Hope was the fifth of how many sons?
Contestant: Four.

Phil Wood Show, BBC GMr.

Wood: What 'K' could be described as the
Islamic Bible?
Contestant: Er...
Wood: It's got two syllables... Kor...
Contestant: Blimey?
Wood: Ha ha ha ha no. The past participle of run...
Contestant: (Silence)
Wood: OK, try it another way.
Today I run, yesterday I...
Contestant: Walked?

Daryl's drive time, Virgin Radio

Daryl Denham: In which country would you spend shekels?
Contestant: Holland?
Denham: Try the next letter of the alphabet.
Contestant: Iceland? Ireland?
Denham: (helpfully) It's a bad line. Did you say Israel?
Contestant: No.

continued...

SUBJECT: SIGNS FOUND IN KITCHENS

1. Kitchen closed – this chick has had it!

2. Martha Stewart doesn't live here!

3. I'm creative, you can't expect me to be neat too!

4. So this isn't Home Sweet Home... Adjust!

5. Ring Bell for Maid Service... If no answer, do it yourself!

6. I clean house every other day... Today is the other day!

7. If you write in the dust, please don't date it!

8. I would cook dinner but I can't find the can opener!

9. My house was clean last week, too bad you missed it!

10. A clean kitchen is the sign of a wasted life.

11. COOK CAN'T TAKE IT ANY MORE!

12. I came, I saw, I decided to order take out.

13. If you don't like my standards of cooking...
    lower your standards.

14. You may touch the dust in this house...
    but please don't write in it!

15. Apology... Although you'll find our house a mess, come in, sit
    down, and converse. It doesn't always look like this: Some days
    it's even worse.

16. A messy kitchen is a happy kitchen, and this kitchen
    is delirious.

17. If we are what we eat, then I'm easy, fast, and cheap.

18. A balanced diet is a cookie in each hand.

19. Thou shalt not weigh more than thy refrigerator.

20. Blessed are they who can laugh at themselves for they shall never cease to be amused.

21. A clean house is a sign of a misspent life.

22. Help keep the kitchen clean – eat out.

23. Countless number of people have eaten in this kitchen and gone on to lead normal lives.

24. My next house will have no kitchen – just vending machines.

SUBJECT: SOMETHING TO OFFEND

Q: What do toilets, a clitoris, and an anniversary have in common?.
A: Men miss them all.

Q: How can you tell the Irish guy in hospital?.
A: He's the one blowing the foam off his bedpan.

Q: How do you get a sweet little old lady to swear?
A: Get another sweet little 80-year-old, to shout, "Bingo."

SUBJECT: SEVEN KINDS OF SEX...

Recent research shows that there are seven kinds of sex:

The first kind of sex is called: Smurf Sex.
This kind of sex happens when you first meet someone and you both have sex until you are blue in the face.

The second kind of sex is called: Kitchen Sex.
This is when you have been with your partner for a short time and you are so horny you will have sex anywhere, even in the kitchen.

The third kind of sex is called: Bedroom Sex.
This is when you have been with your partner for a long time. Your sex has gotten routine and you usually have sex only in your bedroom.

The fourth kind of sex is called: Hallway Sex.
This is when you have been with your partner for too long. When you pass each other in the hallway you both say, "screw you."

The fifth kind of sex is called: Religious Sex.
Which means you get Nun in the morning, Nun in the afternoon and Nun at night.

The sixth kind is called Courtroom Sex.
This is when you cannot stand your wife any more. She takes you to court and screws you in front of everyone

And last, but not least, the seventh kind of sex is called: Social Security Sex.
You get a little each month. But not enough to live on.

SUBJECT: HOW TO SHOWER LIKE A WOMAN

How to Shower Like a Woman

1. Take off clothing and place it in sectioned laundry hamper according to lights and darks.

2. Walk to bathroom wearing long dressing gown.

3. If you see your partner along the way, cover up any exposed areas.

4. Look at your womanly physique in the mirror – make mental note – must do more sit-ups.

5. Get in the shower.

6. Use face cloth, arm cloth, leg cloth, long loofah, wide loofah and pumice stone.

7. Wash your hair once with cucumber and sage shampoo with 43 added vitamins.

8. Wash your hair again to make sure it's clean.

9. Condition your hair with grapefruit mint conditioner enhanced with natural avocado oil. Leave on hair for fifteen minutes.

10. Wash your face with crushed apricot facial scrub for ten minutes until red.

11. Wash entire rest of body with ginger nut and jaffa cake body wash.

12. Rinse conditioner off hair (you must make sure that it has all come off).

13. Shave armpits and legs.

14. Consider shaving bikini area but decide to get it waxed instead.

15. Scream loudly when your partner flushes the toilet and you lose the water pressure.

continued...

16. Turn off the shower.

17. Squeegee off all wet surfaces in shower.

18. Spray anti–mould solution on spots on shower walls.

19. Get out of shower.

20. Dry with towel the size of a small country.

21. Wrap hair in super absorbent second towel.

22. Check entire body for the remotest sign of a zit.

23. Tweeze hairs.

24. Return to bedroom wearing long dressing gown and towel on head.

25. If you see your partner along the way, cover up any exposed areas and then sashay to bedroom.

26. Spend and hour and a half getting dressed.

How to Shower Like a Man

1. Take off clothes while sitting on the edge of the bed and leave them in a pile.

2. Walk naked to the bathroom.

3. If you see your wife along the way, shake dick at her making the"woo-woo" sound.

4. Look at your manly physique in the mirror and suck in your gut to see if you have pects (no).

5. Admire the size of your dick in the mirror and scratch your ass.

6. Fart.

7. Scratch your nuts and smell for the last time.

8. Get in the shower.

9. Don't bother to look for a wash cloth (you don't use one).

10. Wash your face.

11. Wash your armpits.

12. Blow your nose in your hands, then let the water just rinse it off.

13. Crack up at how loud your fart sounds in the shower.

14. Majority of time is spent washing your privates and surrounding area.

15. Wash your butt, leaving those coarse butt hairs on the soap bar.

16. Shampoo your hair (do not use conditioner).

17. Make a shampoo Mohawk.

18. Peek out of shower curtain to look at yourself in the mirror again.

19. Pee (in the shower).

20. Rinse off and get out of the shower.

21. Fail to notice water on the floor because you left the curtain hanging out of the tub the whole time.

22. Look at yourself in the mirror, flex muscles, and admire penis size again.

23. Leave shower curtain open and wet bath mat on the floor.

24. Leave bathroom fan and light on.

25. Return to the bedroom with towel around your waist.

26. If you pass your wife, pull off the towel, shake dick at her, and make the 'woo-woo' sound again.

27. Throw wet towel on the bed.

continued...

28. Get dressed in under two minutes.

29. Fart.

SUBJECT: SECRET WOMAN'S BUSINESS

The female is always correct.

- The rules are subject to change at any time without prior notice.

- No male can possibly know the rules.

- If the female suspects the Male knows all the rules, she must immediately change some or all the rules.

- The female is never wrong.

- If the female is wrong, it is because of a flagrant misunderstanding which was the direct result of something the male did or said wrong.

- If the above rules applies, the male must apologise immediately for causing the misunderstanding.

- The female can change her mind at any given point in time.

- The male must never change his mind without express written consent from the female.

- The female has every right to be angry or upset at any time.

- The male must remain calm at all times, unless the female wants him to be angry or upset.

- The female must under no circumstances let the male know whether or not she wants him to be angry or upset.

SUBJECT: THREE MEN

Three men (a doctor, a lawyer, and a biker), were sitting in a bar talking over a few drinks.

After a sip of his martini, the doctor said, "You know, tomorrow is my anniversary. I bought my wife a diamond ring and a new Mercedes. I figure if she doesn't like the diamond ring, then at least she will like the Mercedes, and she will know that I love her."

After finishing his scotch, the lawyer said, "Well, on my last anniversary, I bought my wife a string of pearls and a trip to the Bahamas. I figured if she didn't like the pearls, then at least she would have enjoyed the trip, and she would have known that I loved her."

The Biker then took a big swig from his beer, and said, "Yeah, well for my anniversary, I got my old lady a t-shirt and a vibrator. I figured if she didn't like the t-shirt, then she could go please herself."

SUBJECT: TEACHER

The teacher brings a statue of Venus into the class and asks, "What do you like best about it class? Let's start with you Robert."

"The artwork" says Robert.

"Very good. And you Peter?"

"Her tits" says Peter.

"Peter get out! Go stand in the hall," responds the teacher

"And you, Johnny?"

"I'm leaving, Teacher. I'm leaving..."

SUBJECT: TEN THINGS MEN UNDERSTAND ABOUT WOMEN

1.

2.

3.

4.

5.

6.

7.

8.

9.

10.

SUBJECT: MY THERAPIST

My therapist told me the only way to achieve true inner peace is to finish what I start.

So far today I have finished, two bags of chips and a chocolate cake. I feel better already.

SUBJECT: THE TEENAGER...

An old man was sitting on a bench at the mall.

A teenager sat down next to him. He had spiked hair that was red, orange, yellow, green, blue and violet.

The old man stared.

Whenever the teen looked, the old man was staring.

Finally, the teenager said sarcastically, "What's the matter, old boy, never done anything wild in your life?"

Without missing a beat the old man replied, "Got drunk once and had sex with a peacock. Just wondering if you were my son."

SUBJECT: TOUGH

"I've just had the most awful time," said a boy to his friends. "First I got angina pectoris, then artheriosclerosis. Just as I was recovering, I got psoriasis. They gave me hypodermics, and to top it all, tonsillitis was followed by appendectomy."

"Wow! How did you pull through?" sympathised his friends.

"I don't know." the boy replied. "Toughest spelling test I ever had."

SUBJECT: TEE HEE

Miss Brooks was having trouble with one of her first grade pupils. "Johnny, what is your problem?"

Little Johnny answered, "I'm too smart for the first Grade. My sister is in third grade and I'm smarter than she is! I think I should be in the third grade too!" Miss Brooks had enough, so she took Johnny to the Principal's office.

The Principal agreed that he would give the boy a test and if he failed to answer any of his questions he was to go back to the first grade and behave. He started by asking Johnny some simple arithmetic.

"What is three times three?"
"Nine, Sir."
"How much is nine times six?"
"Fifty-four."
And so it went with every question the Principal thought a third grade should know the answer to.
The principal looked at Miss Brooks and said, "I think Johnny can go to third grade! He seems smart enough."

Miss Brooks said to the principal, "Let me ask him some questions?" The Principal agreed.

Miss Brooks asked, "What does a cow have four of that I have only two of?"
Johnny, after a moment, answered, "Legs, Ma'am"
"What do you have in your pants that I don't have?"
"Pockets!"
"OK, what does a dog do that a man steps into?"
"Pants."
"What starts with a C and ends with a T, is hairy, oval, delicious and contains thin whitish liquid?"
"Coconut."
"What goes in hard and pink then comes out soft and sticky?"
The principal's eyes opened really wide and before he could stop the answer, Johnny was taking charge. "Bubble gum!"
"What does a man do standing up, a woman does sitting down and a dog does on three legs?"

"Shake hands, Ma'am."

"Now for some 'Who am I?' sort of questions, OK?"
"First one.
You stick your pole inside me, you tie me down to get me up, and I get wet before you do."
Johnny, quick as ever, answered, "Tent!"
"OK, a finger goes in me. You fiddle with me when you're bored. The best man always has me first."
The Principal was looking restless and a bit tense. But Johnny was on the ball with "Wedding Ring!"
"I come in many sizes. When I'm not well, I drip. When you blow me, you feel good."
"Nose."
"Right, I have a stiff shaft, my tip penetrates, and I come with a quiver."
"Arrow."
"Good, now for the last one. What word starts with an 'F', ends in K', and means a lot of heat and excitement?"
"Firetruck, Ma'am!"

The Principal breathed a sigh of relief and said to the teacher,
"Send him to university, I got the last ten questions wrong myself!"

SUBJECT: TOP TEN WAYS TO KNOW IF YOU HAVE PMS...

1. Everyone around you has a attitude problem.

2. You're adding chocolate chips to your cheese omelette.

3. The dryer has shrunk every last pair of jeans.

4. Your husband is suddenly agreeing with every thing you say.

5. You're using your mobile phone to dial up bumper stickers say. "How's my driving?" Call 1-800-EAT-SHIT

6. Everyone's head looks like an invitation to batting practice.

7. You're convinced there is a God. And he's male.

8. You're counting down the days until Menopause.

9. You're sure everyone is scheming to drive you crazy.

10. The Panadol bottle is empty, and you bought it yesterday.

SUBJECT: TRUE

This IS THE transcript of the true and actual radio conversation between a large Military ship off the coast of a small country in 1998. Radio conversation released by the Chief of Naval Operations 10/01/01

Small Country: Please divert your course 15 degrees to the South, to avoid a collision.

Military Ship: Recommend you divert your course 15 degrees to the North to avoid collision.

Small Country: Negative. You will have to divert your course 15 degrees to the South to avoid a collision.

Military Ship: This is the Captain of a British Navy Ship. I say again divert YOUR course.

Small Country: Negative. I say again you will have to divert YOUR course.

Military Ship: THIS IS THE AIR CRAFT CARRIER AND THE LARGEST SHIP IN THE FLEET.
WE ARE ACCOMPANIED BY THREE DESTROYERS, THREE CRUISERS AND NUMEROUS SUPPORT VESSELS. I DEMAND THAT YOU CHANGE YOUR COURSE 15 DEGREES NORTH,
I SAY AGAIN, THAT IS 15 DEGREES NORTH, OR COUNTER MEASURES WILL BE UNDERTAKEN TO ENSURE THE SAFETY OF THIS SHIP.

Small Country: We are a lighthouse. Your call.

SUBJECT: TWO WOMEN

Two women in heaven were discussing how they had died.

"I froze to death, it wasn't so bad. After I quit shaking from the cold, I began to get warm and sleepy, and finally died a peaceful death. What about you?"

"I died of a massive heart attack. I suspected that my husband was cheating, so I came home early to catch him in the act. But instead, I found him all by himself in the den, watching TV."

"So what happened?"

"I was so sure there was another woman there somewhere that I started running all over the house looking. I ran up into the attic and searched and down to the basement. Then I went through every closet and checked under every bed. I kept this up until I had looked everywhere, and finally became so exhausted that I just kneeled over and died of a massive heart attack."

"Too bad you didn't look in the freezer, we'd both still be alive."

SUBJECT: TOTAL SENSE

I've got all the money I'll ever need, unless I buy something.

SUBJECT: THREE MEN

One day, three men were hiking and unexpectedly came upon a large raging, violent river.

They needed to get to the other side, but had no idea how to do so. The first man prayed to God, saying, "Please God give me the strength to cross the river."

Poof! God gave him big arms and strong legs and he was able to swim across the river in about two, hours after almost drowning a couple of times.

Seeing this, the second man prayed to God, saying, "Please God, give me the strength and the tools to cross the river."

Poof! God gave him a row boat and he was able to row across the river in about an hour, after almost capsizing the row boat a couple of times.

The third man had seen how this worked out for the other two, so he also prayed to God, saying, "Please God, give me the strength, the tools and the intelligence, to cross the river."

And Poof! God turned him into a woman. She looked at the map, hiked upstream a couple of hundred yards, then walked across the bridge.

SUBJECT: TOO TRUE

If you're shopping online the boss will come and talk to you!

SUBJECT: THE REAL THREE BEARS STORY

Baby Bear goes downstairs and sits in her little chair at the table. She looks into her little bowl. It is empty. "Who's been eating my porridge?!!" she squeaks.

Daddy Bear arrives at the table and sits in his big chair. He looks into his big bowl and it is also empty. "Who's been eating my porridge?!!" he roars.

Mummy Bear puts her head through the serving hatch from the kitchen and yells, "For Christ's sake, how many times do we have to go through this with you idiots? It was Mummy Bear who got up first, it was Mummy Bear who woke everyone in the house, it was Mummy Bear who made the coffee, it was Mummy Bear who unloaded the dishwasher from last night, and put everything away, it was Mummy Bear who went out in the cold early morning air to fetch the newspaper, it was Mummy Bear who set the damn table, it was Mummy Bear who put the friggin' cat out, cleaned the litter box and filled the cat's water and food dish, and now that you've decided to drag your sorry bear-asses downstairs and grace Mummy Bear's kitchen with your grumpy presence, listen good, cause I'm only gonna say this one more time...

"I HAVEN'T MADE THE DAMN PORRIDGE YET ! ! !"

SUBJECT: TRUTH

The average amount of sleep needed by the average person is ten minutes more than you get.

SUBJECT: THINK ABOUT THIS!

- Laughter is like changing a baby's diaper: It doesn't permanently solve any problems, but it makes thing more acceptable for awhile.

- Live as you wish your kids would.

- Living on Earth is expensive, but it does include a free trip around the sun every year.

- Love is like a rose. You have to see past the thorns to appreciate its beauty.

- Middle age is when broadness of the mind and narrowness of the waist change places.

- Middle age is when you choose your cereal for the fibre, not the toy in the packet.

- No job is so simple that it can't be messed up.

- Some mistakes are too much fun to only make once.

- Support bacteria – they're the only culture some people have.

- The pessimist may be right in the long run, but the optimist has a better time during the trip.

- You can give without loving, but you cannot love without giving.

SUBJECT: THE TWINS

There were these twin sisters just turning one hundred years old in St. Luke's Nursing Home and the editor of the Cambridge rag, '*The Cambridge Distorter*', told a photographer to get over there and take the pictures of these 100-year-old twins.

One of the twins was hard of hearing and the other could hear quite well. The photographer asked them to sit on the sofa and the deaf one said to her twin, "WHAT DID HE SAY?"

He said, "WE GOTTA SIT OVER THERE ON THE SOFA!" said the other.

"Now get a little closer together," said the cameraman.

Again, "WHAT DID HE SAY?"

"HE SAYS SQUEEZE TOGETHER A LITTLE."
So they wiggled up close to each other.

"Just hold on for a bit longer, I've got to focus," said the photographer.

YET AGAIN – "WHAT DID HE SAY?"

"HE SAYS HE'S GONNA FOCUS!"

With a big grin, the deaf twin shouted out, "Me first!"

SUBJECT: GREAT TRUTHS OF LIFE...

- Once over the hill, you pick up speed.

- I love cooking with wine. Sometimes I even put it in the food.

- If it weren't for STRESS I'd have no energy at all.

- Whatever hits the fan will not be evenly distributed.

- If the shoe fits... buy it in every colour.

- If you're too open-minded, your brains will fall out.

- Age is a very high price to pay for maturity.

- If you must choose between two evils, pick the one you've never tried before.

- My idea of housework is to sweep the room with a glance.

- If you look like your passport picture, you probably need the trip.

- Bills travel through the mail at twice the speed of checks.

- A conscience is what hurts when all your other parts feel so good.

- Experience is a wonderful thing. It enables you to recognize a mistake when you make it again.

SUBJECT: AIN'T THAT THE TRUTH

- Never read the fine print. There ain't no way you're going to like it.

- If you let a smile be your umbrella, then most likely your butt will get soaking wet.

- The only two things we do with greater frequency in middle age are urinate and attend funerals.

- The trouble with bucket seats is that not everybody has the same size bucket.

- To err is human, to forgive – highly unlikely.

- Do you realize that in about 40 years, we'll have thousands of old ladies running around with tattoos?

- Money can't buy happiness – but somehow it's more comfortable to cry in a Porsche than in a Hyundai.

- Drinking makes some husbands see double and feel single.

- Living in a nudist colony takes all the fun out of Halloween.

- After a certain age, if you don't wake up aching in every joint, you are probably dead.

- As usual, if you don't forward this to ten of your friends within the next five minutes, your belly button will fall off and you won't get any Irish good luck or surprises after you press send.

SUBJECT: SO TRUE

Antacid (ant-as'-id) Uncle Acid's wife

Antelope (an'-tl-op) How she married my Uncle

Avoidable (a-void'-a-ble) What a bullfighter tries to do

Baloney (B_a-lo'-ne) Where some hemlines fall

Bernadette (Brn'-a-det) The act of torching a mortgage

Bottom (Bot'-em) What the shopper did when she found the shoes that she wanted.

Bucktooth (Buk'-tooth) The going rate for the tooth fairy

Burglarize (Bur'-gler-ise) What a crook sees with

Cantaloupe (kan'-tl-op) When you are unable to run away to get married

Cartoonist (kar-toon'-ist) What you call your auto mechanic

Castanets (kas'-te-net) What they did to fill the role of Frankie Avalon's movie girlfriend

Celtics (sel'-tiks) What a parasite salesman does

Decrease (dee-krees) De fold in de pants

Demote (dee-mot) What de king put around de castle

Despise (dee-spiz) De persons who work for the CIA

Detention (dee-ten'-shen) What causes de stress

Dreadlocks (dred'-lok) the fear of opening the dead bolt

SUBJECT: THIN PEOPLE DON'T...

I read every diet I can get my hands on.

I even follow there suggestions. But eventually, inevitably, I always get fat again. Now, at last, I've found the answer. After living for 14 years with a man who never gains an ounce, no matter what I serve him. I've found out what it is that keeps, him thin. He thinks differently.

The real difference between fat and thin people is that thin people:

- Avoid eating popcorn at the movies, because it gets their hands greasy.

- Split, a thin based pizza, with three friends.

- Think chocolate coated biscuits, are for the kids.

- Think that doughnuts are indigestible.

- Read books they have to hold with two hands.

- Become so absorbed in a weekend project they forget to have lunch.

- Fill the lolly jar on there desk with paper clips.

- Counteract the mid afternoon slump with a nap instead of a Krispy Kreme.

- Exchange the deep fryer they got for Christmas, for a clock radio.

- Lose their appetites when they're depressed.

- Think the Easter Bunnie is for the kids.

- Throw out stale potato chips.

- Will only eat, Swiss or Dutch chocolate, which cannot be found, except in a special store.

- Thinks it's too much trouble to stop at a special store just to buy a chocolate.

- Don't celebrate with cake, when they have lost a pound.

- Warm up after skiing with black coffee, instead of hot chocolate, whipped cream and marshmallows.

- Try all the salads at the buffet, leaving room for only one dessert.

- Find iced tea more refreshing, than an ice cream soda.

- Think banana splits are for the kids.

- Brings four biscuits to the TV room, instead of the whole packet.

- Have no compulsion to keep the lolly jar symmetrical by reducing the jelly beans

- Think that topping apple Danish, with ice cream and whipped cream is too rich.

SUBJECT: NEW TESTAMENT BLOOPERS FROM SUNDAY SCHOOL STUDENTS

- When the three wise guys from the East Side arrived, they found Jesus in the manager.

- Jesus was born because Mary had an immaculate contraption.

- St John, the Blacksmith, dumped water on his head.

- Jesus enunciated the Golden Rule, which says to do one to others before they do one to you. He also explained, "Man doth not live by sweat alone."

- It was a miracle when Jesus rose from the dead and managed to get the tombstone off the entrance.

- The people who followed the Lord were called the 12 decibels.

- A Christian should have only one wife. This is called monotony.

- The epistles were the wives of the apostles.

- One of the opossums was St. Matthew, who was by profession a taxi man.

- When Mary heard that she was the Mother of Jesus, she sang the Magna Carta.

- St. Paul cavorted to Christianity. He preached holy acrimony, which is another name for marriage.

SUBJECT: MORE GREAT TRUTHS...

Kids have learned...

1. No matter how hard you try, you can't baptise cats.

2. When Mum is mad at your Dad, don't let her brush your hair.

3. If your sister hits you, don't hit her back. They always catch the second person.

4. Never ask your three-year-old brother, to hold a tomato.

5. You can't trust dogs to mind your food.

6. Don't sneeze when someone is cutting your hair.

7. Never hold a Dust Buster and a cat at the same time.

8. You can't hide a piece of broccoli in a glass of milk.

9. Don't wear polka dot underwear under your white shorts.

10. The best place to be when your sad is Grandma's lap.

Adults have learned...

1. Raising teenagers is like nailing jelly to a tree.

2. Wrinkles don't hurt.

3. Families are like fudge... mostly sweet, with a few nuts.

4. Today's mighty oak is just yesterdays nut that held it's ground.

5. Laughing is good exercise. It's like jogging on the inside.

SUBJECT: TEN THINGS WOMEN WOULD DO IF THEY HAD A PENIS FOR THE DAY.

10. Get ahead faster in the corporate world.

9. Get a blow job.

8. Find out what is so fascinating about beating the meat.

7. Pee standing up while talking to other men in the urinal.

6. Determine WHY you can't hit the bowl consistently.

5. Touch yourself in public regardless as to how improper it may seem.

4. Jump up and down naked with an erection to see of it feels as funny as it looks.

3. Understand the scientific reason for the light refraction which occurs between a man's eyes and the ruler situated next to his member which causes two inches to be added to the final measurement.

2. Repeat number, nine...

SUBJECT: UNIONS AT WORK

A dedicated Teamsters union worker was attending a convention in Las Vegas and decided to check out the local brothels. When he got to the first one, he asked the Madam, "Is this a union house?"

"No," she replied, "I'm sorry it isn't."

"Well, if I pay you $100, what cut do the girls get?"

"The house gets $80 and the girls get $20," she answered.

Mightily offended at such unfair dealings, the union man stomped off down the street in search of a more equitable, hopefully unionised shop. His search continued until finally he reached a brothel where the Madam responded, "Why yes sir, this is a union house. We observe all union rules."

The man asked, "And if I pay you $100, what cut do the girls get?"

"The girls get $80 and the house gets $20" she replied.

"That's more like it!" the union man said. He handed the Madam $100, looked around the room and pointed to a stunningly attractive blonde. "I'd like her," he said.

"I'm sure you would, sir," said the Madam.

Then she gestured to a 92-year-old woman in the corner, "But Ethel here has 67 years seniority and she's next."

SUBJECT: VIRUSES

The George Bush Virus
Causes your computer to keep looking for viruses of mass destruction.

The John Kerry Virus
Stores data on both sides of the disk and causes little purple hearts to appear on screen.

The Clinton Virus
Gives you a permanent hard drive with no memory.

The Al Gore Virus
Causes your computer to keep counting and re-counting.

The Bob Dole Virus
Makes a new hard drive out of an old floppy.

The Lewinsky Virus
Sucks all the memory out of your computer and then emails everyone about what it did.

The Arnold Schwarzenegger Virus
Terminates some files, leaves, but will be back.

The Mike Tyson Virus
Quits after two bytes.

The Oprah Winfrey Virus
Your 200 GB hard drive shrinks to 100 GB and then slowly expands to re-stabilize around 350 GB.

The Ellen Degeneres Virus
Disks can no longer be inserted.

The Prozac Virus
Totally screws up your RAM, but your processor doesn't care.

The Michael Jackson Virus
Only attacks minor files.

The Lorena Bobbitt Virus
Re-formats your hard drive into a 3.5 inch floppy and then discards it through Windows.

SUBJECT: LACKING IN VISION

George Bush has a heart attack and dies. He goes to hell where the devil is waiting for him.

"I don't know what to do here," says the devil. "You are on my list but I have no room for you. You definitely have to stay here, so I'll tell you what I'm going to do. I've got three folks here who weren't quite as bad as you. I'll let one of them go, but you have to take their place. I'll even let YOU decide who leaves."

George thought that sounded pretty good, so he agreed. The devil opened the first room: in it was Richard Nixon and a large pool of water. He kept diving in and surfacing empty-handed over and over and over. Such was his fate in hell. "No!" George said. "I don't think so. I'm not a good swimmer and don't think I could do that all day long."

The devil led him to the next room: in it was Tony Blair with a sledgehammer and a room full of rocks. All he did was swing that hammer, time after time after time. "No, I've got this problem with my shoulder. I would be in constant agony if all I could do was break rocks all day!" commented George.

The devil opened a third door. In it, George saw Bill Clinton, lying on the floor with his arms staked over his head, and his legs staked in a spread eagle poses. Bent over him was Monica Lewinsky, doing what she does best. George Bush looked at this in disbelief for a while and finally said, "Yeah, I can handle this."

The devil smiled and said, "OK Monica, you're free to go"

SUBJECT: VIRTUE

"Virtue is often the result of insufficient temptation."

SUBJECT: DIARY OF A VIAGRA HOUSEWIFE

Day One.
Just celebrated our 23rd wedding anniversary with not much to celebrate. When it came time to re-enact our wedding night, he locked himself in the bathroom and cried.

Day Two.
Today, he says he has a big secret to tell me. He's impotent, he says, and he wants me to be the first know. Why doesn't he tell me something that I don't know! I mean, he actually thinks that I haven't noticed.

Day Three.
This marriage is in trouble. A woman has needs. Yesterday, I saw a column in *Dear Abby* and burst in tears.

Day Four.
A miracle has happened! There's a new drug on the market that will fix his 'problem'. It's called Viagra. I told him that if he takes Viagra, things will be just the way they were on our wedding night. I think it will work. I replaced his Prozac with Viagra, hoping to lift something other than his mood.

Day Five.
What absolute bliss!!!

Day Six.
Isn't it wonderful. It is difficult to write while he's donning that!

Day Seven.
This Viagra thing has gone to his head. No pun intended! Yesterday at Burger King, the manager asked me if I'd like Whopper. He thought they were talking about him, but I have to admit it's very nice. I don't think I've ever been so happy.

Day Eight.
I think he took too many over the weekend. Yesterday, instead of mowing the lawn, he was using his new friend as a weed whacker. I'm also getting a bit sore down there.

Day Nine.
No time to write, he may catch me.

Day Ten.
Okay. I admit it. I mean a girl can only take so much. To make matters worse, he's washing the Viagra down with neat whiskey! What am I going to do? I feel tacky all over.

Day Eleven.
I'm basically being screwed to death! It's like living with a Black and Decker drill. I woke up this morning hot–glued to the bed. Even my armpits hurt. He's a PIG.

Day Twelve.
I wish he was gay. I've stopped wearing make–up, cleaning my teeth or even washing, but he stills keeps coming after me! Even yawning has become dangerous...

Day Thirteen.
Every time I shut my eyes, there's a sneak attack! It's like going to bed with a Scud Missile. I can hardly walk and if he tries that, sorry' thing again, I'll kill the bastard!

Day Fourteen .
I've done everything to turn him off. Nothing is working. I even started dressing like a nun, but this just seems to make him horny. Help me!!!!!!!!!!!!!!

Day Fifteen.
I think I'll have to kill him. The cat and dog won't go near him and our friends don't come over any more. Last night I told him to go f—k himself and he did.

Day Sixteen.
The bastard has started to complain about headaches. I hope the bloody thing explodes! I did suggest he might try stopping the Viagra and going back to Prozac.

Day Seventeen.
Switched pills but it doesn't seem to have made any difference. Gosh!!!!!!!!!!!! Here he comes again.

Day Eighteen.
He's back on Prozac. The lazy sod sits there in front of the telly all day with remote control in his hand and expects me to do everything for him. WHAT ABSOLUTE BLISS!!!!!!!!!!!!!!!!!!!

SUBJECT: VICTORIA'S SECRET

A husband walks into Victoria's Secret to purchase some sheer lingerie for his wife. He is shown several possibilities that range from $250 to $500 in price, the sheerer, the higher the price. He opts for the sheerest item, pays the $500 and takes the lingerie home. He presents it to his wife and asks her to go upstairs, put it on and model it for him.

Upstairs, the wife thinks, "I have an idea. It's so sheer that it might as well be nothing. I'll not put it on, do the modelling naked and return it tomorrow and get a $500 refund for myself. So she appears naked at the top of the stairs and strikes a pose.

The husband says, "Good Lord! You'd think for $500, they'd at least iron it!"

His funeral is Tuesday.

SUBJECT: THE VET...

Guy takes his pet to the vet.

Put's it up on the table and the vet enters the room, takes one look it and say's he'll have to do some tests. He leaves and comes back with a labrador that sniffs it and barks, then the Vet leaves again. Comes back with a persian cat and the cat just meow's. Vet says, "he'll be fine, you owe me $500."

Guy says, "$500 – what for?..."

"Isn't it obvious, you just witnessed me do a lab report and a cat scan"

SUBJECT: VAN GOGH'S FAMILY TREE

His dizzy aunt .... Verti Gogh

The brother who at prunes .... Gotta Gogh

The brother who worked at a convenience store .... Stop n Gogh

The grandfather from Yugoslavia .... U Gogh

The cousin from Illinois .... Chica Gogh

His magician uncles .... Where-diddy Gogh

His Mexican cousins .... Amee Gogh

The Mexican cousin's American half brothers .... Gring Gogh

The nephew who drove a stage coaches .... Wells-far Gogh

The constipated uncles .... Cant Gogh

The ballroom dancing aunts .... Tang Gogh

The bird lover uncles .... Flamin Gogh

The nephew psychoanalysts .... E Gogh

The fruit loving cousins .... Man Gogh

An aunt who taught positive thinkings .... Way To Gogh

The little bouncy nephews .... Poe Gogh

A sister who loved discos .... Go Gogh

And his niece who travels the country in a vans ...... Winne Bay Gogh

A water bearer had two large pots, each hung on each end of a pole that he carried across his neck. One of the pots had a crack in it, and while the other pot was perfect and always delivered a full portion of water at the end of the long walk from the stream to the master's house, the cracked pot arrived only half full. For a full two years this went on daily, with the bearer delivering only one and a half pots of water to his master's house.

Of course, the perfect pot was proud of its accomplishments, perfect to the end for which it was made. But the poor cracked pot was ashamed of its own imperfection and miserable that it was able to accomplish only half of what it had been made to do.

After two years of what it perceived to be a bitter failure, it spoke to the water bearer one day by the stream. "I am ashamed of myself, and I want to apologize to you."

"Why?" asked the bearer. "What are you ashamed of?" "For the past two years, I have been able to deliver only half my load because this crack in my side causes water to leak out all the way back to your master's house. Because of my flaws, you have to do all of this work, and you don't get full value for your efforts," the pot said.

The water bearer felt sorry for the old cracked pot, and in his compassion he said, "As we return to the master's house, I want you to notice the beautiful flowers along the path." Indeed, as they went up the hill, the old cracked pot took notice of the sun warming the beautiful wild flowers on the side of the path, and this cheered it some. But at the end of the trail, it still felt bad because it had leaked out half its load, and so again it apologised to the bearer for its failure.

The bearer said to the pot, "Did you notice that there were flowers only on your side of the path, but not on the other pot's side? That's because I have always known about your flaw, and I took advantage of it. I planted flower seeds on your side of the path, and every day while we walk back from the stream, you've watered them. For two years I have been able to pick these beautiful flowers to decorate my master's table. Without you being just the way you are, he would not have this beauty to grace his house."

Moral: Each of us has our own unique flaws. We're all cracked pots. But it's the cracks and flaws we each have that make our lives together so very interesting and rewarding. You've just got to take each person for who they are, and look for the good in them. There is a lot of good out there. There is a lot of good in us!

SUBJECT: WIDDLE WABBIT

A precious little girl walks into a pet shop and asks in the sweetest little lisp, "Excuthe me, mithter, do you keep widdle wabbits?"

As the shopkeeper's heart melts, he gets down on his knees so that he's on her level, and asks, "Do you want a widdle white wabbit or a thoft and fuwwy bwack wabbit or maybe one like that cute widdle bwown wabbit over there?"

She, in turn blushes, rocks on her heels, puts her hands on her knees, leans forward and says in a quiet voice,
"I don't think my pet python weally gives a thit."

SUBJECT: THE WIFE'S WORK...
IS NEVER DONE.

One day the man came home from work to find total mayhem at home.

The kids were outside with their pyjamas still on playing in the mud. There was empty food wrappings and boxes all around.

When proceeding into the house, he found an even bigger mess. Dishes on the bench, dog food spilled on the floor, broken glass under the table, and a small pile of sand at the back door.

In the family room he found, strewn with toys, various items of clothing and the lamp shade knocked over. He headed up the stairs, stepping over the toys, to look for his wife. Becoming worried she may be ill, something had happened to her was surprised to find her in bed with her pyjamas on reading a book.

Giving her husband a loving smile asked, "how was your day"

Looking bewildered he asked her, "what happened here today"

Smiling at her husband she says, "You know when every day, you come home from work and asked me what I did today?"
"Yes" he replied.

"Well today, I didn't do it."

SUBJECT: WASTE

One thing you can't recycle is wasted time.

SUBJECT: WEDDING NIGHT

At 85 years of age, Morris marries Lou Anne. A lovely 25-year-old.

Since her new husband is so old, Lou Anne decides that after their wedding she and Morris should have separate bedrooms, because she is concerned that her new, but aged, husband may over exert himself if they spend the entire night together.

After the wedding festivities Lou Anne prepares herself for bed, and the expected, knock on the door. Sure enough, the knock comes, the door opens and there is Morris, her 85-year-old groom, ready for 'action'.

They unite as one. All goes well, Morris takes leave of his bride, and she prepares to go to sleep.

After a few minutes, Lou Anne hears another knock on her bedroom door, and it's Morris. Again, he is ready for 'action'. Somewhat surprised, but nonetheless willing, Lou Anne consents to more conjugal bliss.

When the love birds are done, Morris kisses his bride, bids her a fond good night and leaves.

She is set to go to sleep again, but Morris is back again, rapping on the door, as fresh as a 25-year-old. Ready for more passion. Once again, they enjoy one another.

But as Morris prepares to leave again, his young bride says to him, "I am thoroughly impressed that at your age you can perform so well and so often. I have been with guys less than a third of your age who were only good once. You are truly a great lover, Morris."

Morris, somewhat embarrassed, turns to Lou Anne and says, "You mean I was here already?"

SUBJECT: WISDOM FROM THE KIDS...

How do you decide who you want to marry?
You got to find somebody who likes the same stuff. Like, if you like sports, she should like it that you like sports, and she should keep the chips and dip coming.
ALAN – age ten

No person really decides before they grow up who they're going to marry. God decides it all way before, and you get to find out later who you're stuck with.
KRISTEN – age ten

What is the right age to get married?
Twenty-three is the best age because you know the person FOREVER by then.
CAMILLE – age ten

No age is good to get married at. You got to be a fool to get married.
Freddie, – age six

How can a stranger tell if two people are married?
You might have to guess, based on whether they seem to be yelling at the same kids.
DERRICK – age eight

What do you think your Mum and Dad have in common?
Both don't want any more kids.
LORI – age eight

What do most people do on a date?
Dates are for having fun, and people should use them to get to know each other. Even boys have something to say if you listen long enough.
LYNNETTE – age eight

On the first date, they just tell each other lies and that usually gets them interested enough to go for a second date.
MARTIN – age ten

What would you do on a first date that was turning dour?
I'd run home and play dead. The next day I would call all the

newspapers and make sure they wrote about me in all the dead columns.

CRAIG – age nine

When is it okay to kiss someone?
When they're rich.
PAM – age seven

The law says you have to be eighteen, so I wouldn't want to mess with that.
CURT – age seven

The rule goes like this: If you kiss someone, then you should marry them and have kids with them. It's the right thing to do.
HOWARD – age eight

Is it better to be single or married?
I don't know which is better, but I'll tell you one thing. I'm never going to have sex with my wife. I don't want to be all grossed out.
THEODORE – age eight

It's better for girls to be single but not for boys. Boys need someone to clean up after them.
ANITA – age nine

How would the world be different if people didn't get married?
There sure would be a lot of kids to explain, wouldn't there?
KELVIN – age eight

And the number one favourite is...

How would you make a marriage work?

Tell your wife that she looks pretty, even if she looks like a truck.
RICKY – age ten

SUBJECT: WORDS THAT DON'T EXIST, BUT SHOULD

AQUADEXTROUS
Possessing the ability to turn the bathroom tap on and off with your toes.

CARPERPETUATION
The act, when vacuuming, of running over a string or a piece of lint at least a dozen times, reaching over and picking it up, examining it, then putting it back down to give the vacuum one more chance.

DISCONFECT
To sterilize the piece of candy you dropped on the floor by blowing on it, assuming this will somehow 'remove' all the germs.

ELBONICS
The actions of two people manoeuvring for one arm rest in a movie theatre or aeroplane.

FRUST
The small line of debris that refuses to be swept onto the dust pan and keeps backing a person across the room until he or she finally decides to give up and sweep it under the rug.

PEPPIER
The waiter at a fancy restaurant whose sole purpose seems to be walking around asking diners if they want ground pepper.

PHONESIA
The affliction of dialling a phone number and forgetting whom you were calling just as they answer.

PUPKUS
The moist residue left on a window after a dog presses its nose to it.

TELECRASTINATION
The act of always letting the phone ring at least twice before you pick it up, even when you're only six inches away.

SUBJECT: WHAT A WOMAN

Three men were sitting together bragging about how they had given their new wives duties.

Terry had married a woman from America, and bragged that he had told his wife she was going to do all the dishes and house cleaning that needed to be done at their house. He said that it took a couple days but on the third day he came home to a clean house and the dishes were all washed and put away.

Jimmie had married a woman from Canada. He bragged that he had given his wife orders that she was to do all the cleaning, dishes, and the cooking. He told them that the first day he didn't see any results, but the next day it was better. By the third day, his house was clean, the dishes were done, and he had a huge dinner on the table.

The third man had married an Australian girl. He boasted that he told her that her duties were to keep the house cleaned, dishes washed, lawn mowed, laundry washed and hot meals on the table for every meal. He said the first day he didn't see anything, the second day he didn't see anything, but by the third day most of the swelling had gone down and he could see a little out of his left eye. Enough to fix himself a bite to eat, load the dishwasher, and call a landscaper.

God Bless Australian Women!

SUBJECT: WOMEN

Women are more irritable than men because men are more irritating.

SUBJECT: WEDDING NIGHT

A Chinese couple gets married.

They both work in the same Chinese restaurant and it was love at first sight. She's a virgin and, truth be told, he is none too experienced either. On their wedding night, she cowers naked under the bed sheets as her husband undresses. He climbs in next to her and tries to be reassuring.

"My darring" he says. "I know dis yo firs time and you berry frighten. Pomise you, I give you anyting you want, I do anyting – jus anyting you want. Whatchou want?" he asks, trying to sound experienced. He hopes this will impress his virgin bride.

A thoughtful silence follows and he waits patiently (and eagerly) for her request. She eventually replies, shyly and unsurely, "I want... numba 69."

Now he is caught up in thoughtful silence and eventually, in a puzzled tone, he asks, "You want... Beef wif broccori?"

SUBJECT: WOOHOO!!!

"Doctor, I have developed a problem. Everytime I sneeze I orgasm. What remedy do you recommend?"

"Pepper."

SUBJECT: WISDOM FROM GRANDMA...

- Whether a man winds up with a nest egg, or a goose egg, depends a lot on the kind of chick he marries.

- Trouble in marriage often starts when a man gets so busy earnin' his salt, that he forgets his sugar.

- Too many couples marry for better, or for worse, but not for good.

- When a man marries a woman, they become one, but the trouble starts when they try to decide which one.

- On anniversaries, the wise husband always forgets the past – but never the present.

- The bonds of matrimony are a good investment, only when the interest is kept up.

- Many girls like to marry a military man – he can cook, sew, and make beds, and is in good health, and he's already used to taking orders.

- Eventually you will reach a point when you stop lying about your age, and start bragging about it.

- The older we get, the fewer things seem worth waiting in line for.

- When you are dissatisfied and would like to go back to your youth, remember about Algebra.

- I don't know how I got over the hill without getting to the top.

- Ah, being young is beautiful, but being old is comfortable.

- Old age is when former classmates are so grey and wrinkled and bald, they don't recognize you.

- If you don't learn to laugh at trouble, you won't have anything to laugh at when you are old.

SUBJECT: WISE WOMEN
(YOU GOT TA LUV EM)

"Men are like fine wine. They all start out like grapes, and it's our job to stomp on them and keep them in the dark until they mature into something with which you'd like to have dinner with."

SUBJECT: DON'T WORRY...

According to *Self* magazine, one in four women say they have negative thoughts about their body during sex.

See, why do women worry about these kinds of things? During sex men are probably thinking about some other woman's body anyway.

Don't worry about it.

SUBJECT: ANOTHER WISE WOMEN

Men are like playing with a deck of cards.

You need:
- A Heart to love Him.
- A Diamond to Marry Him.
- A Club to smash his head in,
- and a Spade to bury the bastard!

SUBJECT: WISHFUL THINKING

A woman rubbed a bottle and out popped a genie. The amazed woman asked if she got three wishes.

The genie said, "Nope, sorry, three-wish genies are a storybook myth. I'm a one-wish genie. So... what'll it be?"

The woman did not hesitate. She said, "I want peace in the Middle East. See this map? I want these countries to stop fighting with each other and I want all the Arabs to love the Jews and Americans and vice-versa. It will bring about world peace and harmony."

The genie looked at the map and exclaimed, "Lady, be reasonable. These countries have been at war for thousands of years. I'm out of shape after being in a bottle for five hundred years. I'm good but not THAT good! I don't think it can be done. Make another wish and please be reasonable."

The woman thought for a minute and said, "Well, I've never been able to find the right man. You know – one that's considerate and fun, likes to cook and help with the house cleaning, is great in bed, and gets along with my family, doesn't watch sports all the time, and is faithful. That is what I wish for... a good man."

The genie let out a sigh and said, "Let me see the fu*king map again."

SUBJECT: WHIMSICAL FLIGHT ATTENDANTS

Occasionally, airline attendants make an effort to make the in-flight safety lecture a bit more entertaining. Here are some real examples that have been heard or reported:

"As we prepare for takeoff, please make sure your tray tables and seat backs are fully upright in their most uncomfortable position."

"There may be 50 ways to leave your lover, but there are only four ways out of this aeroplane."

"Your seat cushions can be used for floatation, and in the event of an emergency water landing, please take them with our compliments."

"We do feature a smoking section on this flight. If you must smoke, contact a member of the flight crew and we will escort you to the wing of the aeroplane."

"Smoking in the lavatories is prohibited. Any person caught smoking in the lavatories will be asked to leave the plane immediately."

"Good morning. As we leave Dallas, it's warm, the sun is shining, and the birds are singing. We are going to Charlotte, where it's dark, windy and raining. Why in the world y'all wanna go there I really don't know."

Pilot, "Folks, we have reached our cruising altitude now, so I am going to switch the seat belt sign off. Feel free to move about as you wish, but please stay inside the plane till we land... it's a bit cold outside, and if you walk on the wings it affects the flight pattern."

And, after landing, "Thank you for flying Delta Business Express. We hope you enjoyed giving us the business as much as we enjoyed taking you for a ride."

As we waited just off the runway for another airliner to cross in front of us, some of the passengers were beginning to retrieve luggage from the overhead bins. The head steward announced on the intercom, "This aircraft is equipped with a video surveillance system that monitors the cabin during taxiing. Any passengers not remaining in their seats until the aircraft comes to a full and complete stop at the gate will be strip-searched as they leave the aircraft."

As the plane landed and was coming to a stop at Washington National, a lone voice comes over the loudspeaker, "Whoa, big fella... WHOA"

Here are a few heard from Northwest:
Should the cabin lose pressure, oxygen masks will drop from the overhead area. Please place the bag over your own mouth and nose before assisting children or adults acting like children."

"As you exit the plane, please make sure to gather all of your belongings. Anything left behind will be distributed evenly among the flight attendants. Please do not leave children or spouses."

And from the pilot during his welcome message:
"We are pleased to have some of the best flight attendants in the industry... Uunfortunately none of them are on this flight!"

SUBJECT: A WOMEN

A woman gives birth to a baby at St. Vincent's and, afterwards, her doctor comes in looking very, very, solemn. "I'm afraid I have to tell you something about your baby."

The doctor days, "Well, now, nothings wrong exactly. But your baby is a little different."

"A little bit different? What do you mean?"

"Well your baby is a hermaphrodite."

"AN hermaphra what?"

"An hermaphrodite. It means you baby has the... er... features... of a male and a female."

The young mother is a aghast. She says, "Oh my God. You mean it has a penis and a brain."

SUBJECT: THE PERFECT WAL-MART GREETER

A very loud, unattractive, mean-acting woman walks into Wal-Mart with her two kids in tow, screaming obscenities at them all the way through the entrance.

The Wal-Mart Greeter says, "Good morning and welcome to Wal-Mart. Nice children you've got there. Are they twins?"

The ugly woman stops screaming long enough to say,
"Hell no they aint!
The oldest one, he's nine and the younger one, she's seven.
Why the hell would you think they're twins?
Do you really think they look alike?"

"No," replies the greeter, "I just couldn't believe you got laid twice!"

SUBJECT: WISE WOMEN... CAN'T BEAT THEM

TWENTY DOLLARS:

On their wedding night, the young bride approached her new husband and asked for $20 for their first lovemaking encounter. In his highly aroused state, her husband readily agreed.

This scenario was repeated each time they made love, for more than 30 years, with him thinking that it was a cute way for her to afford new clothes and other incidentals that she needed.

Arriving home around noon one day, she was surprised to find her husband in a very drunken state. During the next few minutes, he explained that his employer was going through a process of corporate downsizing, and he had been let go.

It was unlikely that, at the age of 59, he'd be able to find another position that paid anywhere near what he'd been earning, and therefore, they were financially ruined.

Calmly, his wife handed him a bank book which showed more than thirty years of steady deposits and interest totaling nearly $1 million.

Then she showed him certificates of deposits issued by the bank which were worth over $2 million, and informed him that they were one of the largest depositors in the bank.

She explained that for the more than three decades she had 'charged' him for sex, these holdings had multiplied and these were the results of her savings and investments.

Faced with evidence of cash and investments worth over $3 million, her husband was so astounded he could barely speak, but finally he found his voice and blurted out, "If I'd had any idea what you were doing, I would have given you all my business!"

That's when she shot him.

You know, sometimes, men just don't know when to keep their mouths shut!